How to Make Good Business Decisions

How to Make Good Business Decisions

Dr. J.C. Baker

BEP
BUSINESS EXPERT PRESS
Leader in applied, concise business books

How to Make Good Business Decisions

Copyright © Business Expert Press, LLC, 2021.

Cover design by Charlene Kronstedt

Interior design by Exeter Premedia Services Private Ltd., Chennai, India

First published in 2021 by
Business Expert Press, LLC
222 East 46th Street, New York, NY 10017
www.businessexpertpress.com

ISBN-13: 978-1-63742-064-5 (paperback)
ISBN-13: 978-1-63742-065-2 (e-book)

Business Expert Press Business Career Development Collection

Collection ISSN: 2642-2123 (print)
Collection ISSN: 2642-2131 (electronic)

First edition: 2021

10 9 8 7 6 5 4 3 2 1

Description

How to Make Good Business Decisions is a book to assist people with thoughts surrounding essential aspects of finances and business. Much of the decision-making for people derives from experiences and exposure. The ability to see multiple perspectives allows for a higher level of understanding, increasing common sense perception. The common belief for the concept of common sense is a general acceptance as a usual occurrence or stance among people. However, reality demonstrates that people view topics very differently. Technology and varying media outlets create many avenues for information leading to conflicting positions and confusion.

This book provides a straightforward method of removing distortions among education, business practices, finances, and ownership. There are countless variables, obstacles, and barriers inherent in life's journey, and operating with common sense will alleviate many issues.

However, exposure to information, experiences, and education redefines what is "common." Readers will learn how their thoughts, viewpoints, and focus shape their responses and navigation through important decision-making realities. This book serves as a tool for increasing decision-making.

Keywords

common sense; decision making; education; business; finances; ownership; team building; interdependence; meta-cognition

Contents

Book Overview

How to Make Good Business Decisions

The nine chapters are broken down as follows:

Chapter 1: Introduction

Chapter 2: Train of Thought

This chapter begins the foundation for thought throughout the book. Aspects such as logic, linear reasoning, free thought, meta-cognition, and programmed thought are outlined. Challenging the basis of the origin of a person's thinking process sets the occasion for understanding.

Chapter 3: Straight A's

This chapter explains how all aspects of accomplishment is the product of a process. The common-sense aspect to realize is how to recognize and execute the appropriate procedure for the situation. With an educational analogy, the imagery of process implementation assists with successful thinking.

Chapter 4: Free T-Shirt

This chapter provides detailed insight into the concepts of opportunity cost and risk. In decision making, it is common to face either/or realities. It is also common for people to miss the trade-off associated with making choices. The financial analogy creates a picture of how the lack of forethought can be a substantial cost.

Chapter 5: H$_2$O

This chapter teaches the importance of flexibility, agility, and awareness. People struggle with common realities based on situations, surroundings, or circumstances. Having a mentality to adjust and the willingness to see varying perspectives bodes well for anyone seeking universal success.

Chapter 6: Golden Rule

This chapter speaks to an enhanced version of how to interact with people. The common sense take-away is how to see each connected relationship from a different worldview increasing relational success. The price of poor relationship building is more costly than any other tangible reality.

Chapter 7: Mine or Yours

This chapter outlines ownership and commitment. Commonly, the boundaries ownership are misconstrued and violated. The challenge in this chapter is to reflect on common thoughts surrounding ownership, governance, and responsibility.

Chapter 8: Interdependence

This chapter teaches the importance of understanding the universal law of interdependence among all things. It is common for people to believe that their efforts are individualized and primarily have a personal effect. An inclusive paradigm will lead to increased relational and personal success.

Chapter 9: Why

This chapter is the culmination of how to measure every thought regarding decision making. The "why" of anything governs our position, perceptions, and perceptions. Asking this question surrounding all things increases understanding and wisdom, leading toward a more healthy and inclusive life.

CHAPTER 1

Introduction

How to Make Good Business Decisions is a book to assist people with thoughts surrounding essential aspects of a business. The premise of the book covers common sense or basic sense approaches to all decision-making matters. Conceptually, common or basic sense is simple. I submit that common sense is a complicated philosophy owing to the many layers of personal learning and influence. What is common to one individual can vary significantly to another person. This is undoubtedly the reality in business. A good business decision for a venture capital group is measured differently from that of a nonaccredited investor, even if the criteria for investing are similar. The venture group may weigh the impact on the entire portfolio of investments and other investments they are considering. A nonaccredited investor may weigh the ability to leverage a relationship or participate in an industry of interest.

Much of the decision making for people derives from experiences and external exposure. The ability to see multiple perspectives allows for a higher level of understanding, increasing the perception of common sense. The standard belief for the concept of common sense is a general acceptance as a usual occurrence or stance among a group of people. However, reality demonstrates that people view topics very differently. In today's climate, there are many avenues for information leading to conflicting positions and confusion. This book provides a straightforward method of removing distortions among education, business practices, finances, and ownership. There are countless variables, obstacles, and barriers inherent in the journey of life, and operating with a strong philosophical base alleviates many issues. However, exposure to information, experiences, and education redefines what is "common" and constitutes good decision making. This work highlights how people's thoughts, viewpoints, and focus shape their responses and navigation through important decision-making realities. This book serves as a tool for increasing the essential business acumen for all people.

The decision-making process is not an in-the-moment action but the culmination of continued thought over a life-span. Family dynamics, educational training, past experiences, personal characteristics, responsibility level, and outcome expectations are variables attached to decision making. These characteristics are the same for a person's baseline for common- or basic sense. The aspects of decision making explored in this work are not connected to business ethics but to prevailing thoughts surrounding basic concepts. If a business owner seeks to make a budgetary decision for a company, this decision derives from the individual's perspective about money, risk tolerance, impact to the company, retribution back to the decision maker, and the obligation to the company. Each one of these factors carries the weight of previous perspective programming for the individual.

Many business owners and division leaders experience failure due to the inability to make quick, simple, and sound decisions. The common- or basic sense aspects of decision making increase with repetition, information, knowledge, and understanding. Elements such as fear, ignorance, pressure, and hope are factors of poor decision making. Therefore, good decision making for business owners comes from intentional thought and decision practice. The sum of progress and growth extends from the ability to make and manage decisions at the fundamental level. Just as the case in athletics, acting, or the arts, the phrase perfect practice makes perfect applies to decision making. Decision making is a skill that has to be practiced, measured, and analyzed. The fundamentals of good decision making are a product of practice in a particular realm. As a Business Doctor and the CEO of a global consulting firm, I witness the errors and the genius of business owners around the world. One common aspect is that barriers, obstacles, and decision making intertwine the daily operations of companies and small businesses alike.

Fundamentally, making good decisions is the most critical element for sustainability and longevity. To speed up the process of good decision making is the product of common sense leaning on muscle memory from practice, problem recognition, and the understanding of the range of results. Making a future decision is directly connected to past programming. A healthy knowledge of previous choices, coupled with well-thought-of goals, sets the occasion for sound decision making. Recognizing how you think and how those thoughts connect to other aspects is a significant step in increasing decision-making skills.

Chapter 2, Train of Thought, begins the foundation for thought throughout the book. Aspects such as logic, linear reasoning, free thought, meta-cognition, and programmed thought are outlined. Challenging the basis of the origin of a person's thinking process sets the occasion for understanding. Discovering the rationale as to how you process your thoughts and interpret experiences is necessary for viewing decisions in the proper perspective. Establishing a core concept, primary product, or generating ideas, processes, and services extend from how information and thoughts are processed. The train of thought is a natural course of thinking governing the overall decision making for a person.

Chapter 3, Straight A's, explains how all aspects of accomplishment are the product of a process. The common-sense aspect to realize is how to recognize and execute the appropriate procedure for the situation. With an educational analogy, the imagery of process implementation assists with successful thinking. The following chapter Free T-Shirt, provides detailed insight into the concepts of opportunity cost and risk. In decision making, it is common to face "either this/or that" realities. It is also common for people to miss the trade-off associated with making choices. The financial analogy creates a picture of how the lack of forethought can be a substantial cost.

The H_2O chapter teaches the importance of flexibility, agility, and awareness. People struggle with every-day realities based on situations, surroundings, or circumstances. Having a mentality to adjust and the willingness to see varying perspectives bodes well for anyone seeking universal success regardless of climate. The Golden Rule chapter speaks to an enhanced version of how to interact with people. The common sense take-away is how to see each connected relationship from a different worldview increasing relational success. The price of low relationship building is more costly than any other tangible reality. Decision making increases once relational dynamics are understood and accepted.

The chapter entitled Mine or Yours outlines ownership and commitment. Commonly, boundaries of ownership are misconstrued and violated. The challenge in this chapter is to reflect on common thoughts surrounding ownership, governance, and responsibility. Following this is the chapter titled Interdependence. This chapter teaches the importance of understanding the universal law of interdependence among all things. It is common for people to believe that their efforts are individualized and primarily have a personal effect. An inclusive paradigm will lead to increased relational and personal success.

The final chapter, Why, is the culmination of how to measure every thought regarding decision making. The "why" of anything governs our position, perspectives, and perceptions. Asking this question surrounding all things increases understanding and wisdom, leading toward a more healthy and inclusive life.

Business owners and prospective owners face either life-changing or business-changing decisions daily. Working to get a business to market involves decisions in personal finances, career aspirations, family implications, and time management. Launching a new product includes decision making surrounding budget restraints, opportunity costs, employee welfare, branding considerations, and company sustainability. Each chapter contributes to the enhancement of increased decision making through intentional analysis of common sense.

CHAPTER 2

Train of Thought

Definition of Logic—The science of the formal principles of reasoning.

Synonyms—Intellection, reason, sense. (Dictionary.com)

Definition of Linear—Involving a single dimension. Of the first degree with respect to one or more variables.

Synonyms—Straight, direct. (Collins English Dictionary)

Definition of Meta-cognition—Higher-order thinking that enables understanding, analysis, and control of one's cognitive processes, especially when engaged in learning.

Definition of Reason—Statement offered in explanation or justification. Rational ground or motive. Sufficient ground of explanation or of a logical defense. Thing that makes some fact intelligible.

Synonyms—Rationale, explanation. (Online Etymology Dictionary)

The definitions mentioned here create the framework for the goal of the book. Determining if a decision is a good or bad one stems from the perspective of what is logical, what are the reasons, and the string of actions leading up to the decision. The perception of a decision's soundness connects to the rationale and the pre-thoughts of the decision maker. The initial challenge is to determine if people's logic and justification are a product of individual creation, evolution, adaptation, or a planned purpose.

The train of thought exists as the linear thinking model a person employs in decision making. The train of thought does not begin during the moment of decision making but throughout time and connected with experiences, trauma, successes, comfort, and historical results. All these aspects contribute to the decision-making ability of a person, especially during intense decision-making scenarios. An individual's consistent behaviors, personal bias, comfort, and the ramifications to the outcome combine creating the path for choice selection. A person must be conscious of their historical programming and current reality when making business decisions.

The historical programming comes from other related thinking patterns and should not be viewed as isolated choice making. A person's train of thought interconnects with beliefs and views about their inherent and conscious decision-making style. Design thinking speaks to cognitive, strategic, and practical processes used in a multitude of contexts extended from natural to business operations. Divergent thinking is a method of thinking used to produce ideas by exploring many possible solutions in an uncoordinated manner. Design thinking is more calculated planning, while divergent thinking is an intentional creative process. Brainstorming includes aspects of both design and divergent thinking. The practice, procedure, method, tools, heuristics, and approach all provide the framework for identifying and solving problems needed for good decision making.[1]

Weighing the benefits and the risks of a decision happens automatically in some cases and intentionally in others. The conscious decision-making process takes practice and purposeful integration into the train of thought. Ideation and meta-cognition serve as a precursor for good decision making and should be regarded as a premium in daily operations. Cognitive biases such as the hindsight bias, positive illusions, social exchange, and error management theory help bridge the paradox of why consistent variation in thinking style does not necessarily lead to similarly consistent differences in cognitive biases.[2] Different aspects of bias, unintentional thought, illusions, and thinking styles drive preferences of how to think compared to a person's actual behaviors involving judgments and decisions.[2] This reality of decision making governs all choice execution, including business decisions.

The role of analytic thinking in comparison to a holistic thinking style compares linear view with worldviews. Holistic thinkers are more likely to perceive that multiple factors, instead of a single element, may contribute to the development of an event, encouraging them to consider both critical and less critical information. Analytic thinkers are affected mainly by the crucial factors in decision making, pointing the concentration of decision making to a focal point.³ An appointed leader or a business owner needs to demonstrate a sound knowledge of their thinking style to understand the ramifications of their decisions appropriately. Without mastery and comprehension of one's thinking style, the consistency in decision making is lost, leaving the manifestation of decisions left to chance. Good decision making is not based on the outcome but the process to arrive at the result. The thinking process used determines the percentages of good decision making.

The thinking process of decision making should be revered over the "gut-feeling" or intuitiveness way of making decisions. People's intuition is often incorrect, and it is often difficult for people to revise their thinking.⁴ This statement is not to say that instincts do not play a factor in decision making, but using an impulsive method of decision making as a primary tool leads to inconsistency and uncertainty. Good decision making is a perpetual act with reasoning to support the position. A business owner lives in the existence of trial and error because of the numerous variables inherent in the business climate. The thinking process prepares the business owner for the various obstacles allowing for a higher percentage of success in decision making. There are four principles common to many design-thinking approaches:

1. Observe and notice
2. Frame and reframe
3. Imagine and design
4. Make and experiment.⁴

The four principles provide a framework for actively outlining the parameters for conscious decision making. Design and divergent thinking processes benefit from the four principles as a holistic approach are utilized, and the practice of these principles sets the occasion for an established habit. The more a decision-making process is used, the quicker a decision can be made. Employing a process does not denote time delays or multiple decision-making stages. The overarching concept is to identify your process, bias, skillset, and culture while recognizing the ramifications, risks, and rewards of the decision at hand.

Automotive Thinking

For example, to illustrate this initial challenge, let us consider buying or leasing a vehicle. Some people believe that a smart financial decision is only purchasing a car in cash or paying off the vehicle through an aggressive purchase plan. Some people think that a vehicle should never be bought because it is a depreciating asset; therefore, leasing is a smarter decision. Some people do not have a definitive opinion on one side versus the other side. With the three given outcomes, how does someone determine which is a good or a bad decision? What is rational, logical, or common sense? The answer to if it is a good decision to buy a vehicle or not is "Yes" and "No." The answer depends on a host of factors that can be viewed as rational or irrational when connected to the full scope of variables or, in other words, the train of thought. The linear view of this question begins with analyzing all the known connected aspects, including the following:

1. Is the vehicle for personal or business use?
2. What is the credit grade for the purchaser?
3. What is the historical vehicle behavior of the purchaser?
4. Is the vehicle seen as a service or an asset?
5. Is the purchaser seeking future adjustment options with the vehicle?
6. Is there a prospective family or business ramification?
7. Are there write off implications?
8. Is the purchaser trading a previous vehicle?
9. Is the vehicle used as a credit tool?
10. Is the vehicle needed for short-term or long-term use?

All of these aspects change the position of decision making. Any combination of these questions plays a role in altering the perception of the decision and the common-sense modality. Some financial celebrities advocate avoiding leasing a vehicle at all costs, and the only appropriate choice is to purchase a vehicle free and clear. It is reasonable to execute a plan involving the elimination of debt. However, there are instances where debt is useful to reduce tax obligations or leverage dollars for exponential gain. For example, if a person seeks to eliminate as much debt as possible and own a business, the scrutiny of dollars becomes a premium.

Instead of paying $4,000 as a down payment, a $450 monthly payment, and adding additional payments to pay off the auto loan aggressively, it may be more advantageous to save the down payment, lease the same vehicle for $300 a month and reinvest the extra money into a new product launch earning 10x in your business. Conversely, instead of leasing a new car at $400 a month on a 10k mile per year agreement, it may be more advantageous to purchase an older model vehicle in cash with a service contract for $8,000 due to the minimal driving and a short commute. This decision is a $6,000 financial gain to the vehicle buyer with an owned asset that can be leveraged if needed to be.

Although there are complicated ways to determine if purchasing a vehicle is a good decision or a bad decision, there are undeniable common reasons for buying a vehicle. Common causes include an instance when an engine fails in the current automobile, the personal credit file is low, and the decision is to accept the only available option presented by the dealership. This decision is not made in isolation but rather as a string of previous decisions manifesting as a direct causal effect on the current choice. A person's past decision making creates the framework for future decisions, thus reducing the concept of a "good" or "bad" decision but simply forcing the only existing alternative. This new alternative sets the occasion for new decision making carrying the same impact as the historical decisions. In other words, the effect of a low credit file stemmed from preceding decisions. Purchasing another vehicle, working to pay this vehicle aggressively, and working on a credit boosting program allows for a better future decision opportunity. This purchase and pay strategy is the employment of linear thought, increasing the reasoning skill of the person, and demonstrating meta-cognition.

Elements of Persuasion

When analyzing the train of thought, the concept speaks to onset identification. We must travel back to determine if our thinking happens by way of evolution, adaptation, or planned manipulation. I submit that the train of thought occurs in a combination of all three aspects, but people are mostly affected by planned manipulation. It is reasonable to believe that people self-generate their conclusions about the world, their place in the world, and how they interact in the world. Many legitimate examples suggest that people experience manipulation by consensus, authority, and consistency. These aspects are three of the six elements of persuasion used to assist people with decision making. The complete list of the six features of persuasion is as follows:

1. Consensus
2. Consistency
3. Authority
4. Reciprocity
5. Liking
6. Scarcity.[5]

These persuasive elements are present in conversation exchange throughout our life. These aspects represent how we accept advice from family members, receive guidance from a teacher, make purchasing decisions, or simply follow instructions from a superior. A person's train of thought begins with the introduction to these elements and the results of the collective experiences. The outcomes are weighed based on expectations, which reflects on the elements of persuasion.

For example, a father can exert "authority" over a child when the child is young, pushing the decision making for the child. If the father does not display "consistency" in his actions or relation throughout their life, then the "authority" can be minimized, creating rebelliousness. The child grows older and declares that they do not "like" the instructions offered by the father due to the "inconsistent" behavior. Others may speak negatively of the father, demonstrating "consensus" that the father has a lessened value. Now, the child has an increased risk factor caused by bad decision making if the decision is connected to the father's position. The father may advise a particular business or financial practice that may be a good decision by all objectionable measures. However, the diminished "authority," lack of "consistency," negative "consensus," and the "dislike" will persuade the child to make a bad objectionable decision to spite the father or simply rebel. In this instance, the child's train of thought was an evolutionary process based on circumstance and emotional stimulus. The decision making connected to any aspect of the father will be misguided, therefore changing the "common-sense" approach.

Influential Decision Making

Manipulation is a crucial component within the train of thought for people setting the precedence for what is common. Manipulation is made possible through a construct called Idealized Influence. Transformational Leadership is a leadership style created by Bernard Bass and Bruce Avolio. Transformational Leadership consists of four constructs:

1. Inspired Motivation
2. Idealized Influence
3. Individual Consideration
4. Intellectual Stimulation.[6]

The Idealized Influence construct determines that influence is an internal aspect that is molded by external factors. For instance, if a person wants to play sports, and there is no direct access to participate, that person will still enjoy recreation sports but may never go on to play collegiately or professionally. The desire to play allows for interaction with recreational sports or fandom. If a person is not interested in sports, all the access to the higher-level competition does not persuade them to participate. In the event they engage in the sport, it is often out of obligation, discontinuing once there is no longer a mandate. Authority figures, sales professionals, governance, media, and appointed leaders can use Idealized Influence to accomplish a goal among the masses. This reality directly affects a person's ability to execute decisions in their best interest. To further highlight this point, I will use three very different examples to establish a common basis.

As a biblical example, the Book of Genesis chapter three verses 1–13 tell the story of the fall of the characters Adam and Eve.

> 1 Now the serpent was more subtle than any beast of the field which the Lord God had made. And he said unto the woman, Yea, hath God said, Ye, shall not eat of every tree of the garden? 2 And the woman said unto the serpent; We may eat of the fruit of the trees of the garden: 3 but of the fruit of the tree which *is* in the midst of the garden, God hath said, Ye shall not eat of it, neither shall ye touch it, lest ye die. 4 And the serpent said unto the woman, Ye shall not surely die: 5 for God doth know that in

the day ye eat thereof, then your eyes shall be opened, and ye shall be as gods, knowing good and evil. 6 And when the woman saw that the tree *was* good for food and that it *was* pleasant to the eyes, and a tree to be desired to make *one* wise, she took of the fruit thereof, and did eat, and also gave unto her husband with her; and he did eat. 7 And the eyes of them both were opened, and they knew that they *were* naked; and they sewed fig leaves together, and made themselves aprons.

8 And they heard the voice of the Lord God walking in the garden in the cool of the day: and Adam and his wife hid themselves from the presence of the Lord God amongst the trees of the garden. 9 And the Lord God called unto Adam, and said unto him, Where *art* thou? 10 And he said, I heard thy voice in the garden, and I was afraid, because I *was* naked; and I hid myself. 11 And he said, Who told thee that thou *wast* naked? Hast thou eaten of the tree, whereof I commanded thee that thou shouldest not eat? 12 And the man said, The woman whom thou gavest *to be* with me, she gave me of the tree, and I did eat. 13 And the Lord God said unto the woman, What *is* this *that* thou hast done? And the woman said, The serpent beguiled me, and I did eat.

The passage explains that instructions came from God, but the serpent in conversation with Eve challenged those same instructions. The manipulation of thought happened in the first verse when the serpent stated, "Did God really say?" This statement created doubt and confusion among Eve. The train of thought for Eve is derailed, and a new decision enters. The serpent makes a declaration in verses four and five and states, "You will not surely die … For God knows that when you eat from it, your eyes will be opened, and you will be like God knowing good and evil." Eve takes the statement and connects the words of the serpent to her physical senses. Verse six reads, "When the woman saw that the fruit of the tree was good for food and pleasing to the eye, and also desirable for gaining wisdom, she took some and ate it." The serpent initiated the manipulation, but Eve controlled the decision making. The Idealized Influence is on display as Eve's decision is directly connected to what she wanted, "liked," and expected. The serpent was able to manipulate those aspects based on Eve's influences. The decision to eat the fruit was against God's authority but was in line with her internal desires regardless of the ramification of the decision making.

Academic Decision Making

As an academic example, we examine the concept of going to college. Many people debate the validity or usefulness of college regarding the return on investment. There is an argument that many influential and successful people have not completed or even attended college. Prevailing research indicates that 66 percent of people with student loan debt from $20,000 to $35,000 report that incurring the debt was not worth it.[7] The same studies demonstrated that 100 percent of individuals paying over $200,000 in student loan debt stated that the debt was not worth it. From a pure decision-making standpoint, the responses and the idea of debt alone are persuasive factors not to attend college.

Historical data supports that bachelor's, and even more, postgraduate degrees yield higher income for people from all demographics. The average household income with a degree over the previous 30 years is $45,000, while the average person with a high school diploma over the same span has been a steady $30,000 annually.[8] If a person is simply considering the financial statistic of income generation, then choosing to attend college would be the better choice.

Using the train of thought, the decision to go to college stems from family backgrounds, future expectations, career desires, and personal preferences among a litany of other factors. The decision to go to college may be purely financial or reflect social aspirations. For instance, my purpose for choosing to attend college was to play football and enter the NFL as a professional football player. My decision to earn a Masters and a Doctorate was motivated to enhance my firm J.C. Baker & Associates, the Business Hospital. None of my direct family members on either side of the family had earned a college degree. I decided to attend college in elementary school, and every action through my undergrad studies was simply the management of that decision. Considering the idea of college was placed in me by my parents at a young age, the goal of a full scholarship was a conscious decision by middle school. The decision to pursue a postgraduate degree was motivated by understanding business models, distribution channels, branding, and sales. The knowledge to leverage my postbaccalaureate degree was made simple as I had a plan to monetize my degree and reduce the financial burden.

Many students decide on college without linking every variable associated with attendance. The common practice of attending college as grade "13" after high school can prove to be a good or bad decision, with only the outcome serving as the determining factor. Measurement of good or bad decisions stems from conscious and deliberate thought derived from meta-cognition with weighted factors to consider. Asking more comprehensive questions about what factors lead you to college and paying tuition or becoming an entrepreneur or employee out of high school assist with better decision making.

Economic Decision Making

As an economic example, let us consider retail and shopping persuasions. Department stores, grocery stores, e-commerce, and other retail outlets benefit from the consumer's train of thought connected to emotion, need, and marketing. Making a purchasing decision can be a minor decision or a major decision depending on the item, money spent, and the impact. Retail sales account for two-thirds of the U.S. economic output.[9] Much of this retail spending purchases through the use of credit cards. Credit card debt has surpassed $4 trillion, and over 42 percent of consumers pay their credit card bills late.[10] The appetite for credit cards has not been reduced even with the average credit card interest rate for good credit hovering at approximately 17.3 percent.[11] Many economists advocate the power of personal debt to fuel economic expansion through available credit, and the demand for consumer goods increases domestic production and economic growth.[12] The decision making for the consumer to make purchasing decisions exist beyond the purchase but stems from the perception and values surrounding money and debt.

Retailers understand the purchasing mentality of consumers and assist in the buying cycle through sales strategies and advertising. Findings suggest that retailers use variety as a competitive tool to reduce the cost of searching and to facilitate a rise in prices on the within-store margin through increased searched costs among brands to create a perceived generalized value.[13] In other words, the retailers reduce the amount of comparative shopping and create a psychological pull to persuade consumers to purchase. This strategy directly attacks the decision-making process of a consumer.

Another example of a retail strategy is Costco's "treasure hunt" approach to in-store merchandising involving shuffling staple items to different locations forcing tempting triggers to purchase additional items.[14] Chemicals associated with joy and love are released by the human brain when discovering new things, which is a tactical strategy to persuade decision makers.[14] Grocery stores employ strategic techniques to convince the buyer as well. The concept of an oversize grocery basket lures shoppers to purchase more than what is needed because of feelings to fill the shopping cart.

All these aspects demonstrate how other factors can interrupt a person's train of thought. The power to understand the internal decision-making process is a great asset. However, the meta-cognition needed to execute the control over decision making is not a common reality. To make a good decision today, a person has to be conscious of previous decisions, the impact of the recent decisions, and the ramifications of the current decision-making opportunity. Decision making is an intentional skill that must be practiced and nurtured.

CHAPTER 3

Straight A's

The train of thought is a reflection of a lifelong process. This process exists consciously or subconsciously. One fundamental aspect of good decision making is the development of a process. The common-sense element of this portion of the train of thought is to recognize the appropriate procedure for a situation and properly execute it. All forms of accomplishment undergo some level of repetitive process. Making a sandwich, brushing teeth, writing a poem, or creating a business result from a process. Practicing meta-cognition and decision-making skills is also a process. The element of critical thinking is a major portion of the decision-making process. It is common for many of our thoughts to arrive from subconscious realities connected to experiences. Intuition and feelings can easily manipulate decision making without a systematic process. Intentional critical thinking includes aspects such as point of view, purpose, problem solving, analysis of information, formed concepts, current assumptions, possible conclusions, and the recognition of consequences.[1] The identification of each element increases the odds of making a good decision as opposed to a bad decision due to the recognition of variables associated with the decision. The decision-making process would become habitual through muscle memory with the reinforcement of the practice.

The habitual exercise of the critical thinking process is not the same as having a decision-making process on "autopilot" as the steps to create the process are active and deliberate. Processes have direct and actionable steps with prescribed procedures governing the strategic position. The overarching purpose of a process is to minimize errors and increase the percentage of accomplishing the articulated goal. The process acts a fail-safe for uncertainty and along with trial and error. Entrepreneurs are influenced by their environmental context leading toward more increased trial and error. The variables connected to entrepreneurship are unpredictable and uncertain for many reasons, including market conditions, resources, and sufficient human capital. Many of the existing critical thinking models do not include constructs or factors such as the environment of the problem in decision-making framework, institutional and socio-cultural environment, ignorance, doubt, cognitive structures, and the person's background.[2] These gaps derive from a failure to adopt a process perspective while utilizing a process that enables the exploration of considerable variables such as contexts and relevant anticipation.[2] In other words, working through a process prepares a person for natural outcomes and obvious opportunities leading toward better decision making.

Decision-making processes shape a person's response to decision outcomes. The expectation of the decision outcome extends from the effort put forth to make the decision. For a person to accept a decision, they must feel that the procedures used to make the decision matched the ramifications of the decision, the process is complete, and the other variables are known. Conversely, when people perceive decision-making procedures as inadequate, unfair, or inferior, they are much less inclined to accept the decision.[3] The goal is to create a process with proven methods to yield the desired results. Creating a process will take trial and error, but the mechanics are controlled with intentional scrutiny to improve the process. The implementation of this process emphasizes the steps of decision making, allowing for more proactive behavior. Business owners benefit from taking an upfront stance on decision making, allowing them to work more efficiently, confidently, and effectively.

Letter Getting Process

I remember coming home from school in the 3rd grade from Mrs. Robinson's Class at Crary Elementary in Detroit, Michigan, with my report card. This is the first report card that I remember receiving, and I am sure that my father still has it in my childhood home. That report card had all "A's" and one "B," which was in Library. I was good at Oregon Trail but not the Dewey Decimal System. I distinctly remember my Dad looking at my report card and saying, "Good job, son," as he patted me on the head like a puppy. Other classmates would receive gifts for their achievement, and my reward was the head pat or the simple acknowledgment.

As a child, my father's reward system was confusing, as I could not determine the lesson he was teaching me, or there was a lesson at all. Although my father was passionate about my overall success in life, I learned that his value did not connect to the grades I received. Later I learned that he connected to the effort, the lessons I learned, and the mastery of concepts. My consciousness of "letter getting" became overt, and I quickly learned that school was a process. Every report card from the 3rd grade through middle school was straight A's. This history of "letter getting" earned me a reputation as being "smart," especially since I did not go to the same school twice until my 8th-grade year, spanning two states and three cities. Many people make the statement, "You must have been smart to get good grades or earn a Doctorate." My response to them is that you must understand the process of getting good grades to earn an advanced degree.

The process of earning an "A" in a primary or secondary school became as easy as a three-step dance. If a student has perfect attendance, turns in every assignment, and asks two questions a day, then there was no way that the student could fail even if they failed every test. This process would land a "C" or better. If you add marginal intelligence or understanding of the subject, then an "A" would follow. I witnessed this practice for 30 years as a student, a parent, and an educator at all four levels. Executing this process is a form of early meta-cognition integrated into the train of thought. This level of decision making also falls into the realm of good business decisions as education carries immense economic and career ramifications.

As an all-state high school football player and track runner, I earned an athletic scholarship to the University of Cincinnati. However, my academic success was the determining factor for every school that offered a full scholarship. My concept of straight A's saved over $70,000 in school-related and living expenses as a business decision. Eliminating college debt allows for more freedom in future decision making regarding career goals, risk-taking, and opportunity costs. In hindsight, the decision to learn the process of "letter getting" manifested as a good decision and set the standard for attaining goals.

As a college student, I did not execute the same gameplan for "letter getting," but I did perform the same train of thought regarding processes.

I graduated with a 2.4-grade point average with my Bachelor's degree in History. This grade point average caused my coaches to classify me as an underachiever, and my family questioned if I was "really" smart or just better than the other students in the Detroit Public School system. My consciousness surpassed "letter getting," and I began to focus on credit hours, real-world experience, and career choices. The decision was to simply "pass" the course with the awarded three credit hours and spend the extra time training, working, or setting up future opportunities. As a married college student, the priority of earning income increased over study sessions. The lure of professional football was ever-present. Gaining professional work experience and networking became a priority as well. There was no satisfaction obtaining an "A" when my other actions could result in a football contract, a raise on my paycheck, or learning how to navigate a room of business professionals.

Conceptually and literally, the time and energy earmarked for non-academic activities proved to be the most valuable academic lesson learned as I used the same acquired skills to parlay a Masters in Business Administration and Doctorate in Business and Organizational Leadership. My 2.4-grade point average was not acceptable when I applied for grad-school 15 years after my undergraduate completion. However, admittance was granted because of my extensive business resume, quality references, and demonstrated business knowledge. I graduated with both postgraduate degrees in under four years with a combined 3.9-grade point average because of the same process I executed in elementary school. My academic advisors at Northcentral University warned against taking two degrees at once and doubling the Doctoral program. I walked my advisor through my process of completion, coupled with their process as an educational institution. The process for my postgraduate work was simple. Considering I was successful in business for nearly 20 years, all of the material studied on both levels was within the scope of work that I had mastered in my career. I turned in every assignment punctually with the exact specifications instructed. I avoided complex theory slowing my progress and focused on aspects that highlighted my strengths. The advisor agreed with my train of thought, and "consistency" was the element of persuasion. This decision proved to be a good business decision as I saved tens of thousands of dollars in tuition and was able to increase my consulting firm's pricing as my credentials increased. Dr. J.C. Baker is worth more than J.C. Baker, which became a significant portion of my business model. Some clients had to pay an increased retainer due to the acknowledged expertise and title change.

Initial Business Decision Making

The straight A's academic example provides a common-sense example of how to accomplish a goal based on a process. However, the train of thought is demonstrated throughout the decision-making stages. To submit to a process is also a demonstration of meta-cognition and comprehensive thinking. When creating a business, there is a process for success and achievement, just like academics. My postbaccalaureate education was made easier owing to the use of skills and experience I mastered over my life, and operating a business is very similar. As the owner of a global consultancy (The Business Hospital), I find that many business owners fail too quickly or struggle too long because their business's foundation derives from poor decision making. Frequently, entrepreneurs decide to start a business because they "dislike" their current job or want to make money. They are convinced by what they "like" or "dislike," which is an element of persuasion, and they do not activate meta-cognition regarding the process of completion. The legal formation of the business, the company's value proposition, and the execution of the process are critical determinants of a healthy business. An owner's business will fail, and they will call the company a bad decision. The decision to create a business is not bad in isolation. The train of thought governs the reality of the decision. Starting a company without the appropriate team, capital, or operational set up is a recipe for a bad decision. The process of making business ownership a good decision begins with not just a business plan but a viability study, financial reserves, the ability to monetize, and a dedicated team. These five aspects serve as an initial process for business creation and set the foundation for good business decision making.

The academic example illustrates how a process led to consistent achievement. Executing a structured process for the company, an internal controls process to govern, a sales process to scale the business, and the adjustment process for re-evaluation leading to sustainability is paramount.

The first decision a business owner has to make is to create a process or follow a process created by a professional. Decision making always carries risk, but a certified process helps minimize errors and increase efficiency. No plan or process can guarantee absolute certainty but provide a framework for guidance. In entrepreneurship, many standard views support a business plan but eliminate execution plans. Business plans outline the work a business owner prepares to accomplish. Execution plans govern the tasks and operations to maximize performance.

Motivation and Expectation

Having a comprehensive plan leads to the creation of a process. The goal is to implement a process as a foundational action as opposed to trial and error, serving as the primary action. It is common for a new business owner to create a business plan or even pay a professional for a business plan. The new business owner soon learns that a business plan is not the same as an execution plan, viability or feasibility study, or a decision-making process. Each of these aspects analyzes different aspects of the business ownership timeline. A business plan tells the business owner how to get to the moon using vibranium from Wakanda. However, the plan is not viable or feasible because vibranium and Wakanda do not exist. Even with a viability or feasibility plan, without an execution plan to govern the daily behavior, the results will be randomized without a point of comparison. The decision-making process governs the business owner's overall actions and sets the baseline for all behaviors. In some cases, the decision-making process acts as a rule book or a guideline for risk-taking, and timely determinations. For instance, operating agreements create a built-in process for company expense choices. There are parameters on how much an employee or an appointed leader can spend on travel, equipment, services, and other business-related items. These guidelines reduce the impact of bad judgment by creating a ceiling on price points, timeframes, and frequency of financial decision making. When a large purchase is needed, the decision makers have to consciously and deliberately discuss the ramifications of the financial need. The operating agreement set the occasion for good decision making in this particular instance.

Business owners may react similarly to students in that they engage in financial behavior, hoping to "find themselves." They invest in business aspects without understanding what they should expect from the investment or even leverage the investment to their benefit. This line of thinking permeates throughout education and entrepreneurship. Creating a plan without a process leaves an individual confused and lost when circumstances do not manifest as desired. For instance, planning for a marathon without a formal training process and a shoe-tying process creates an enormous barrier for completing the marathon. The process of "letter getting" in the concept of straight A's speaks to the intentional thought and duplicated action to gain a result. The process begins with the expectation of the result. If the goal is to get an "A" in a class, understanding the process of school and grades bodes well for success. If the goal is to complete the course with the necessary credit hours for progression, then comprehension of the class requirements is paramount. If the business goal is to replace current W-2 income, then a financial analysis with assumptions and forecasts assists with good decision making regarding the transition into entrepreneurship. Outlining the revenue and distribution channels contribute to good decision making.

Let us continue to examine new business creation for first-time entrepreneurs. Many new business owners create a business owing to a myriad of factors. Some of the most common reasons for starting a business include self-sufficiency, flexibility, control environment, help others, and pursue a passion.[4] All of these reasons are admirable but will not determine the ultimate success of the business. These aspects are attached to emotion, belief, and desire. These factors are related to perseverance and "stick-to-itiveness," which are vital but irrelevant without a process connected to a sound plan. As the new business owner embarks on the journey of entrepreneurship, the owner's intensity reduces as barriers and obstacles arise. The process provides a daily focus leading toward the expected end. Therefore the process replaces the attention placed on barriers but tasks allowing for completion.

Soliciting consumers and business development is a staple of survival for any company. The decision to sell, market, or advertise happens naturally for a business owner. However, the sales, marketing, or advertising process for a business owner is a deliberate action. The sales process for a business owner is a set of habitual actions executed daily to drive revenue. The decision to create or implement a sales process is the initial step. Determining how many steps in the sales process is another decision. Managing the sales cycle process is another decision. Executing the daily sales cycle process is another decision. The business owner's decision about the sales process encompasses other decisions to ensure that the original decision to implement a process is good. Business owners tell others about their business through different channels such as "word of mouth," flyers, e-mail campaigns, and billboards. Each of these broad avenues of solicitation creates awareness for the business but may not follow a process. These awareness activities can be isolated communication attempts providing random results. Random results set the occasion for bad decision making through the manifestation of weak data. The motivation to spread awareness about the business decreases when the engagement does not increase. Lower engagement creates discouragement and disconnection from the original motivation. The new expectation is that people are not interested in the newly formed business leading to a decision to pivot the message or close the business. From a social media standpoint, a business owner thinks it is common sense to make a social media post about their business. The posts are topics, images, and messages that the owner deems important and hopes that the followers appreciate. Many business owners that I work with express the importance of a strong social media presence but neglect to create a process reflecting the importance. Having a posting calendar creates a deliberate action for an expected result. The calendar should be a common-sense action but often overlooked owing to the lack of a formal social media process and goal. The social media process begins with a baseline, platform understanding, target audience, tailored messaging, goal setting, frequency, relevance, and content mix.[4] Developing a process for social media engagement provides stability and consistency. The process allows a business owner to pinpoint which posts yield more traction and connectivity among the base. The results allow for better decision making, conversion, and adjustment. The daily decision is merely following the process, knowing the result generates more trackable consumer engagement. This engagement is measurable over time, producing a metric for future decision making. The implemented social media process gives more information to the business owner, in turn, allowing for an owner to pinpoint the issues with the messaging and pivot the communication for better engagement. Instead of feeling discouraged and disconnected, the business owner is engaged and informed.

Operating under a process has an obvious and common-sense feel, but I submit that early business owners often overlook an intentional process. The decision to implement a sound process governs future decisions minimizing distractions and uncalculated risk. The reduction of distractions and risk also contributes to fewer overall decisions to make. The fewer number of decisions leads to better decision making. Eliminating future decisions removes risks and the opportunity for bad decisions. Therefore, the proactive work of creating and using a process saves time and energy later. Implementing a process from the onset serves as a safeguard for the future. Pointing back to the "letter-getting" process, attending school daily, asking a few questions, and turning in every assignment also govern my nonacademic activity responsibility to follow processes. The goal to achieve was the motivation behind the process and set an expectation of achievement. This process ensured a good return on higher-education investment and time utilization.

Continuous Improvement

Improving processes have been a focal point of businesses since the onset of ownership. There are many process concepts that companies and consultants use to increase the productivity of a business. Many of these processes exist as a philosophical decision by appointed leadership to help the business operate more effectively. From a common-sense standpoint, working to make a company better is a fundamental decision, but determining how to make a business better is complex. Selecting a process derives from experience, research, recommendation, or guidance. The decision-making process includes all forms of selection and should match the ability to execute. The current and future resources for execution, the human capital, and the industry, and the expected outputs directly affect the ability to improve a process. For many entrepreneurs, the thoughts surrounding a continuous improvement process is merely to survive. Considering the volatile nature of new company creation, small business owners work long hours and many days just to generate revenue on a given day. The consciousness to continuously improve gets lost and forgotten through the focus to complete pressing tasks. This reality is where the cliché "working in the business" and "not working on the business" derives. Long-term success comes from working on aspects in the business that can be improved to maximize operational efficiency, profit, conversion percentages, and eliminate waste. The business owner must be conscious of a continuous improvement process daily to improve decision making and the livelihood of the business.

Processes to advance an operation manifests in several ways. Some of these ways include refining the culture, revamping the value proposition, and analyzing the services. Companies make decisions to operate in a lean manner to reduce waste to realize a higher profit. A process to assist with a lean operation is value stream mapping (VSM) found in manufacturing, but proven helpful in other enterprises as a visual mapping technique to optimize and improve systems and processes by reducing redundancies.[5]

Value Stream Mapping

1. **Process activity mapping:** Establish process flows, identify waste and redundancies, and analyze workflow and business processes.
2. **Supply chain response matrix:** Identify any roadblocks in the process using a simple diagram.
3. **Production variety funnel:** Look to other competitors and industries to see what solutions they've discovered for similar problems.
4. **Forrester effect mapping:** Create line graphs that illustrate customer demand against production to visualize supply, demand, and possible delays.
5. **Quality filter mapping:** Identify any defects or problems in the supply chain.
6. **Decision point analysis:** Determine the push-and-pull demand in the supply chain, a process to determine production orders based on either inventory or customer demand.
7. **Physical structure mapping:** A top-down overview of what the supply chain looks like at an industry level.[5]

Kaizen is a Japanese term that is commonly interpreted as "continuous improvement" and translated as "good change." The purpose of Kaizen is to identify where processes break down and where problems originate, finding the cause, and creating a remedy for the root. In the Kaizen philosophy, even leaders need to be prepared to find their own mistakes and address them using the Kaizen principles.[6] Utilizing the Kaizen philosophy focuses on small continuous changes leading to effective results with few major changes. The impact is to reduce large decision making and to reduce the effects of bad decisions. Kaizen is typically a large enterprise focus, but small business owners and entrepreneurs can learn and grow from Kaizen's philosophical integration. Measuring the small changes and capturing the small daily wins builds momentum for a company. This momentum creates a habit of good decision making leading to a tidal wave of success. A million small steps will carry a person many miles. Kaizen's concept is to make small incremental changes and decisions to increase the organization's operation.

The Five S of Kaizen:

1. **SEIRI** - Sort out. Label items as Necessary, Critical, Most important, Not needed now, and Useless.
2. **SEITON** - Straighten. Easy selection of tools. First In, First Out (FIFO).
3. **SEISO** - Shine. Clean and inspected workplace.
4. **SEIKETSU-SEIKETSU** - Standardization. Best practices and written standards.
5. **SHITSUKE** - Sustain. Training and daily execution.[7]

Six Sigma is another process-driven method used to increase the productivity of businesses. Six Sigma creates value for enterprises by identifying defects to be corrected. This method is usually referred to as the tool of total quality management and lean management, whereas it is an independent quality improvement tool that works perfectly well in parallel to other systems, and it can be used efficiently by both production and service-based enterprises. The Six Sigma methodology applies not only to production processes but also in all areas of an organization,

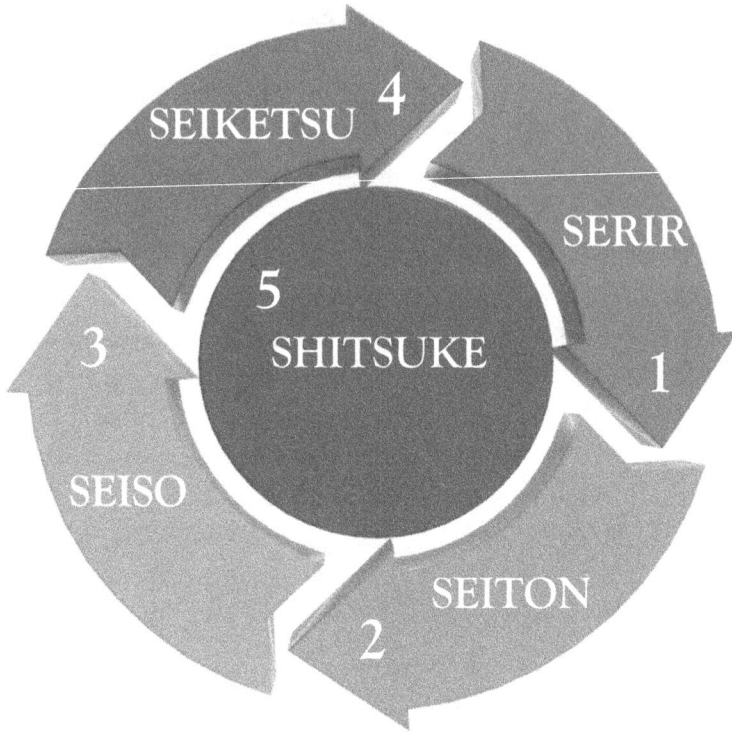

Figure 3.1 Five S of Kaizen[8]

ranging from administration to finances, for output optimization, and performance improvement steps to be significant.[9] Six Sigma is a formal process led by certified and qualified individuals. There is a process to learn the process of Six Sigma. Large companies lean on Six Sigma methods for operational efficiency, reduce waste, and maximize profits. The investment into Six Sigma guidance is a financial decision made by appointed leadership to improve the operational outputs continuously. Business owners can demonstrate good decision making by hiring a certified Six Sigma instructor or taking classes themselves.

Highlighting the DMAIC methodology as a rule for business owners will increase decision making because the categories create a guideline for operations. Even if a business owner is not certified in Six Sigma or has not taken process creation classes, the DMAIC methodology forces specific thoughts about the business and outlines a five-step process for decision making.

DMAIC methodology:

- Define
- Measure
- Analysis
- Improve
- Control[10]

Lean management is often connected to Kaizen and Six Sigma because it merely means to cut down or make the management process slimmer. There are numerous areas in a business worth considering when deciding on how to improve. The organizational structure, responsibility of the personnel, and waste elimination are prevalent aspects of consideration.[12] Many business owners believe "bigger is better" when it comes to offering their services or products. Doing the basics brilliantly is a decision-making stance allowing for a lean mindset when executing the business. For instance, if you are a restaurant owner, having a smaller menu with items that are recognizable to your establishment, controlled costs, maximized profit, and consistency in delivery is a better value proposition

Define	Step 0	Select a Project
Measure	Step 1 / Step 2	Establish Performance Parameters / Validate Measurement System for 'Y'
Analyze	Step 3 / Step 4 / Step 5	Establish Process Baseline / Define Performance Goals / Identify Variation Sources
Improve	Step 6 / Step 7 / Step 8	Explore Potential Causes / Establish Variable Relationship / Design Operating Limits
Control	Step 9 / Step 10 / Step 11	Validate Measurement System for 'X' / Verfiy Process Improvement / Implement Process Controls

Figure 3.2 DMAIC methodology[11]

LEAN MANAGEMENT
Lean Thinking

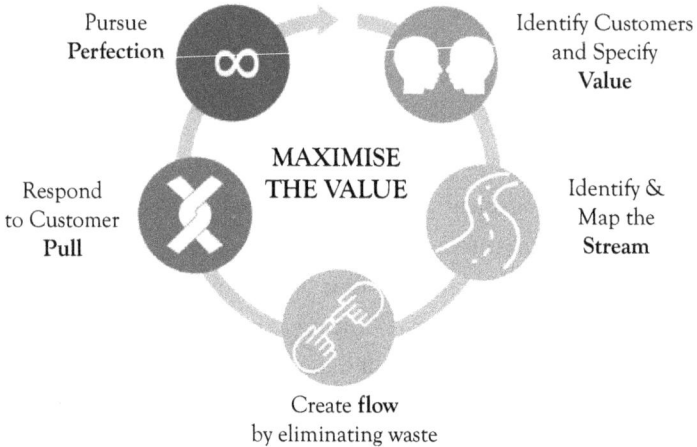

Figure 3.3 Lean management lean thinking[13]

than a larger menu. A larger menu causes confusion in pricing, availability, consistency, and profit analysis. Larger restaurant chains can boast larger menus due to process allowing for growth, experimentation, and customer diversity. A new restaurant does not have the same luxuries in audience recognition, wholesale ability, and process management. Operating on a lean model is a good decision practice for micro- and boutique business owners.

The outline of the named processes is to create a baseline for common-sense practices among large corporations and successful businesses. Each process provides an expectation for the desired end. Business owners need to establish a process to govern the overall decision-making process. Practicing and managing decisions are better than carrying out isolated choices with unanticipated consequences. The example of Straight A's is the demonstration of achievement as a result of a practiced process leading to future successes. The educational process of obtaining "A's" was unchanged but continuously improved on for 35 years. Completing elementary school was the same process as graduating from high school and obtaining a doctoral degree. In terms of business life span, the same 35-year operation is exceptionally successful as nearly 34 percent of small businesses fail within their first two years, according to the Small Business Administration.[14] The train of thought suggests that process creation and implementation increases the chances of sustainability and thus serving as a good business decision. Practicing a process also increases the common-sense level surrounding continued decision making.

CHAPTER 4

Free T-Shirt

I have heard the saying, "The best things in life are free." I imagine when this phrase speaks to walks in the park with a loved one, lying in bed with your infant child, watching a sunrise, or having a snowball fight. Each one of those activities does not cost a penny to perform, and they leave lasting memories. However, when we speak of free, it generally comes with a connotation of obtaining something. That something could be getting an object, a service, or a benefit. The truth that is not apparent when given an object or service for "free" is that it comes with a price. Sometimes that price is so heavy you would have been better off paying for the free item and forfeiting the cost.

This same concept is applied when people speak of owning a company and being their own boss. The general belief is that they are not obligated to work for anyone and that they are the rule-makers. Entrepreneurs soon discover that they become slaves to the business, and other governing bodies take control of their lives, such as the Internal Revenue Service and the legal system. The trade-off from earning a paycheck for the time spent is the sacrifice of stability for uncertainty. The cost of uncertainty comes in many forms, such as low credit scores, debt, stress, and limited free time. It is common to underestimate the obligations and responsibilities inherited by a business owner. Many people make decisions that place them in bondage, which is the idea of the free T-Shirt.

Opportunity Cost

I visit the international amusement park Cedar Point in Sandusky, Ohio, regularly since my youth. I go to the park for the thrill of the roller coasters, and I do not spend much time playing games to win the prizes. When I see people excited about the prize they won, I think to myself, "Look at the prize they purchased." I know that they technically won the prize by throwing a ring over a bottle or hitting a balloon with a dart. I also understand that the point of the game is the challenge and excitement over achieving the goal and winning the prize. However, they literally bought it because they spent $20 on a $0.62 teddy bear. There is a monetary cost involved, not to mention the cost of comfort for carrying the enormous teddy bear around the amusement park or renting a locker. This concept is no different from instant lottery tickets people play at their local gas station. They will complain about the rising gas prices but ignore the fact that they spent $15 on "scratch-offs" therefore inflating their gas price. The challenge in the train of thought is not the anticipation of winning but genuine belief that they are actually "winning." The thought process is that they received something of higher value than what they paid. The decision to gamble provides the illusion of investing. This illusion is the foundation for the revenue models of casinos. The "House," which is the common referral of casinos, always wins, and people have committed financial ruin in the belief that they will win against the "House."

There is an opportunity cost to everything we do. High school seniors and first-year college students learn about opportunity costs in Economics class to add to the foundation of financial common sense. There is something to give to obtain something of value in every scenario. The object we give up determines if we have value in what is provided. The object that we offer includes but is not limited to money, time, information, or access. The opportunity cost is the dynamic worth recognizing and used as the basis for good decision making.

I attended undergrad on a full athletic scholarship, and many people referred to this scholarship as a "full-ride." I commonly referred to my scholarship as a paid work-study, creating confusion in people and leading to dialogue. People's train of thought did not allow them to see that the scholarship caused me to forfeit freedom as well. Every decision was either directed or scrutinized by the university. Coaches dictate class schedules in favor of practice, workouts, study table, travel, and games. Violation of any aspect could result in dismissal from the team and revocation of the scholarship or what others would refer to as the "free ride." My opportunity cost is trading the free will of decision making in exchange for the opportunity to play the sport and have my education paid. This reality is no different from a person enrolling in the military to have their college tuition paid. They would not receive free tuition but paid for the education with their service, hence the term work-study.

Opportunity is determined by the realization of available options in a given circumstance. How a person views an opportunity comes from the conscious deliberation of the presented choices. The idea that choices alter preferences has been widely studied in psychology, yet prior research has focused primarily on options for which all alternatives were salient at the time of selection.[1] The opportunity costs capture the value of the best-forgone alternative and should be considered part of any decision process, yet people often neglect them. The prominence of opportunity costs should be highly regarded at the time of choice with careful evaluation of all the available options.

Event shortfall is a composite of implementation shortfalls and portfolio shortfalls—a measure of the opportunity cost incurred between the time the investment decision is made and the execution benchmark. When these two measures are taken together, an asset owner has a better understanding of the total cost of a reallocation event—that is, the full risk—from the decision to completion. The bottom line is that there is risk in waiting to implement an investment decision that can diminish or even eliminate the perceived benefits of the reallocation decision.[2]

Appreciating and realizing opportunity costs is an internal exercise. People determine what aspects of a decision are valuable, and their worldview dictates the recognition of that value. For instance, spending money to take a vacation before paying the rent is an internal value proposition by the individual. The importance of vacation is a priority over the responsibility to the landlord. The perceived or realized satisfaction of the vacation trumps the need for the good standing with the landlord, avoiding an eviction notice, or preserving credit. The trade-off becomes a direct competitor of the dichotomy of choices, and the train of thought takes over for the person.

It is also true that people view choice constraints as external when the necessity to trade off one option for another relates to extraneous resource limitations such as whenever time, budget, or space constraints necessitate choosing between two desirable offers.[3] Economic theory argues that opportunity costs should be weighed equally to other costs; prior research has indicated that consumers often underweigh or even neglect opportunity costs.[3] An intentional mentality toward identifying opportunity costs tends to be undervalued, creating negative consequences, and more failed opportunities. The owner does not realize the benefit of progress in the manner initially believed due to a lack of understanding. The result manifests in regrets or remorse due to the purposeful or accidental oversight of the pros and cons of the decision making. The process of analyzing the opportunity costs needs to be established in the muscle memory through the train of thought.

A basic premise of people's mentality is that decisions are made in what is believed to be in the best interest of self. Expressly, Expectancy Theory assumes that beliefs can explain human action that one's actions will lead to successful outcomes.[4] The perceived consequence or benefit of the activities leads to the popularity of Expectancy Theory and outlines the entrepreneurs' optimism. As I work with business owners around the world, the common thread among their belief systems is that their concept, company, or competitive offering is superior or unique. Business owners and entrepreneurs alike struggle with the downside of their business models and plans. The opportunity cost for embarking on a project or company creation is frequently missed with grandeur ideas connected to the hopeful success of the business venture. Just as with the college freshman example, the interest payments, fees, and amortization schedule of the credit card are not challenged when obtaining the card in exchange for the free T-shirt.

Following this train of thought, startup founders and business owners place effort in venture creation with the belief of high-level achievement. A startup founder asks for a $250,000 investment in a pitch meeting from an angel investor because their idea is worth $20 million based on their personal assessment. They also request the money because they believe they can execute a $20 million operation without anyone else's help, even with a lack of experience. This train of thought is common due to the Expectancy Theory and the perceived belief of success. The mean outcome of entrepreneurial effort is negative, suggesting that entrepreneurs may be behaving irrationally, which plagues many small business owners.[4]

As a direct example, my company J.C. Baker & Associates—The Business Hospital, engaged in a joint venture partnership with a manufacturing company. Members of my company wanted to purchase equity in the company because of the opportunity for financial gain, long-term success, and the microtransaction potential. As a formal step, we discussed all of the negatives surrounding the joint venture and the ramifications of the opportunity costs. The two members of my company changed their mind and decided to act as contractors to the company and not owners. The negative aspects of ownership in the space were beyond their understanding and control factors, making the opportunity an extreme risk for them.

On the other hand, the opportunity cost for my participation was meager and limited due to the internal controls, experience, and previous success in the space. Included in the train of thought are discovery, evaluation, and exploitation. In my company, we view these actions as the Assessment, Diagnosis, and Business Physical. The examination allows for the careful deliberation of the boundary conditions, action ramification, overall awareness, and the associated opportunity costs.

Free Shirt Comes with a Price

The truth about opportunity cost brings me to the concept of the free T-Shirt. As grade school focused on primary academic topics such as history, math, science, and English, neglecting issues such as finances and life skills. Life skills are categorized as topics needed for real-world scenarios. Traditionally, students who are considered "at-risk" or have disabilities participate in life skills classes. This classification of life skills classes covers aspects such as grocery shopping, public transportation, and self-sufficiency skills. Financial literacy is an essential life skill in the United States as a result of capitalism. A new paradigm surrounding life skills is needed to include high-level financial literacy from primary school. Including financial literacy at an early age would reset what is considered common sense and imbed good financial decision making into the train of thought. Instead, many college students learn these lessons on college campuses, altering their future decisions.

Students and parents alike look forward to the college experience with the expectation of a life-improving journey. Often these dreams can be deferred based on the free T-Shirt received in the first semester of school. In exchange for the free T-Shirt, students provide their credit information. The linear thought process takes precedence over what should be a common-sense decision, and the student submits the credit information for the gift. The credit card is then used, maxed out, and defaulted. Couple this credit decision with student loan debt, and the excitement of the college experience becomes frustration and resentment. The average student loan debt is over $31,000, with a payoff time of up to 30 years for the average student.[5] The free T-Shirt is not the reason behind the economic and credit woes, but it is a vehicle leading to bad economic decisions. It is reasonable to believe that the train of thought leading to the free T-Shirt selection is the same thought process employed in other financial matters. How a person weighs risk regarding opportunity costs is a formal process, just like any other major decision.

Personal Decisions Are Business Decisions

Many view credit as an internal dialogue reserved for families. The issue with this train of thought is that the country's economy operates by specific financial principles pertinent to all people regardless of culture and views. A person's credit report determines purchasing power, work opportunities, and insurance risk. Financial disaster accompanies a lack of proper understanding of money and economics. As crucial as topics such as supply and demand are essential for a business owner, such issues as credit, finance, and taxes are proven to impede business progress and cause failure. With a history of credit repairs, mortgage short-sales, and financial health analyses, I witness issues crippling business owners and people in general from bad decision making. Marriages fall apart because of money problems, homelessness because of money mismanagement, depression from the inability to get finances under control, and suicide because of the burden of debt. Although aspects such as marriage and mortgages appear personal, they are directly proportional to business. Decision making is not an isolated act but an interdependent phenomenon connecting all matters of life. The opportunity costs for personal life as a value in business and vice versa. The free T-Shirt as a college sophomore can prevent a person from opening a business a decade later due to insufficient capital and the inability to leverage credit. The amount of debt carried from a failed marriage or a tax obligation can create rejections on equipment, or vendor terms needed to operate a business successfully. The train of thought is to understand the pros and cons of every decision and weigh the risk versus reward. As a business owner, the daily decisions intertwine without separation, so the business becomes a lifestyle choice. Recognizing this opportunity cost reminds the business owner to lean on the process and remember the overall purpose of the goal.

Investment Tolerance

Another popular term in business is "It takes money to make money." I heard this statement numerous times throughout my life, and I was unable to appreciate the cliché until I created my first company CIG Management LLC two decades ago. Unlike the free T-Shirt, where the opportunity cost is giving up something of value in return of something of lower value, the investment operates as the reciprocal. Business owners have to develop a tolerance for investing in their business to achieve growth. The negative connotation regarding higher education is the exuberant costs and potential debt associated with college. The other side of this reality is the investment the student is making in developing themselves formally. If leveraged appropriately, the investment can yield high dividends. Statistically, individuals holding a degree earn significantly more than those that do not. A person with a high school diploma earns nearly $50,000 less in the United States than a person with a bachelor's degree.[6]

These numbers indicate that the opportunity costs of debt serve as a motivating factor to generate more income over a person's lifetime. This train of thought points to attending college as a good decision assuming leveraged appropriately as a business decision. Leveraging the decision is attached to the execution plan, Expectancy Theory, and the recognition of opportunity. Attending college and graduating does not equate to the higher lifetime earnings but the deliberate action of exploiting possibilities within the scope of individual strengths. Learning from mistakes, errors, and failures are vital for future success, minimizing the opportunity costs for decision making.

Business owners face challenging decision-making opportunities regularly. Many business owners can immediately acknowledge the need for a tool or equipment to perform their service or create their product. This rationale is embedded into the common-sense thinking of business owners. A restaurant owner logically understands the need for a stove, a kitchen hood, and a commercial freezer. That same business owner may

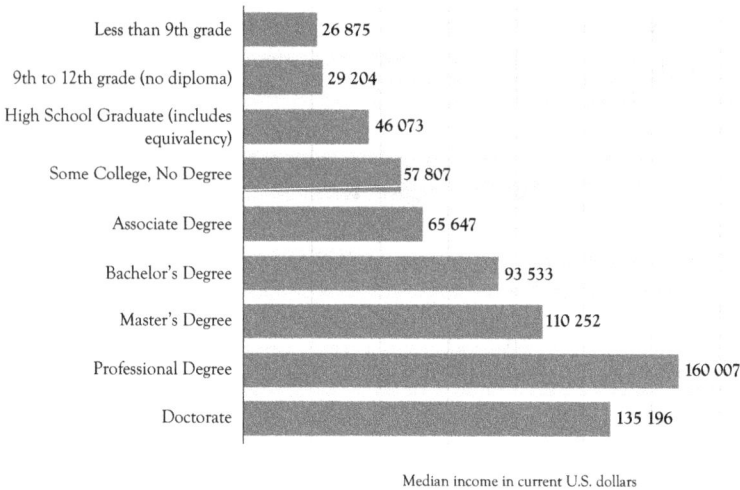

Median income in current U.S. dollars

Figure 4.1 Median income in dollars[7]

have difficulty understanding the need for a consultant to assist with strategy, execution, and trend analysis. The investment into learning more about the industry or the internal operation may not be as appealing. Not investing in knowledge, information, and access can prove to be a costly error for business owners. Owing to the inexperience of the business owner, the opportunity costs associated with the lack of a professionally constructed execution plan is a premature failure. In many cases, the business owner does not have enough information or knows the appropriate questions to ask to generate an accurate assessment for the opportunity costs. Entrepreneurs have the feeling of good decision making based on their worldview and passion toward the business, but the lack of information surrounding their endeavor leads to mistake and error. The separator is the ability to withstand early mistakes, persevere, and turn the trials into lessons of learning. In some cases, the opportunity costs from errors can be too significant to rebound, leaving permanent damage to the business.

The graph illustrates that the first ten reasons for failure are topics covered by management consultants with expertise in those matters. The business owner may not have any experience or classical training in any of the aspects. The lack of investment to save money cost the business owner, proving to be a bad decision. The train of thought could exist from the precedence of "do it yourself" to reduce costs or the adage,

The Top Reasons Startups Fail
Most frequently cited reasons for startup failure*

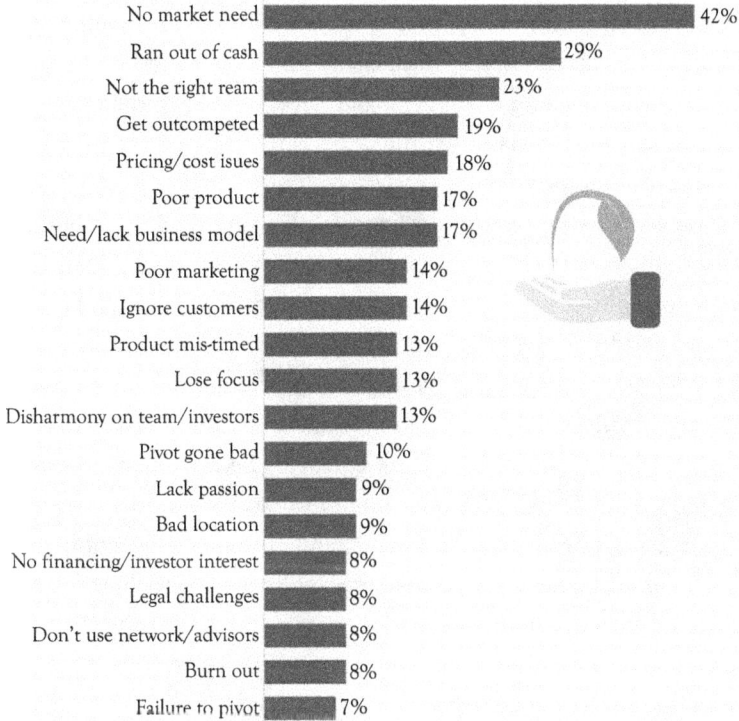

Reason	Percentage
No market need	42%
Ran out of cash	29%
Not the right ream	23%
Get outcompeted	19%
Pricing/cost isues	18%
Poor product	17%
Need/lack business model	17%
Poor marketing	14%
Ignore customers	14%
Product mis-timed	13%
Lose focus	13%
Disharmony on team/investors	13%
Pivot gone bad	10%
Lack passion	9%
Bad location	9%
No financing/investor interest	8%
Legal challenges	8%
Don't use network/advisors	8%
Burn out	8%
Failure to pivot	7%

* Based on an analysis of 101 startup post-mortems
@StatistaCharts Source: CB Insights

statista

Figure 4.2 The top reasons startups fail[8]

"If you want something done right, you do it yourself." The restaurant owner could be great at cooking and very poor at market segmentation, budgeting, and human capital management. In this instance, the free T-Shirt is the belief that investing in the learning of the business or the industry was not a significant value. The opportunity costs became the loss of the company and failure.

The first reasons for company failure are "no market need" and "ran out of cash," indicating poor preparation and misdiagnosis. There is a market for nearly every product, service, or organization type. The goal is to create the company in a recognizable, accessible, and affordable way for the selected target audience. The target audience might be smaller than imagined initially, but even a small market can sustain a micro- or boutique business. Business owners also have to learn how to articulate their offerings to their pointed audience. If the business owner is not proficient in messaging, placement, and conversion, then the manifestation appears as "no market need." Business owners must consider a range of factors when launching a company and have a strong command of the opportunity costs associated with their offering.

The same is to be said for the aspect of "running out of money." Small business owners struggle with the financial element of running a business owing to the miscalculation or unintentional ignoring economic strategy. The opportunity costs connected to sustainability in a market are not adequately considered when not formally calculated. The financial categories related to business ownership typically supersedes the knowledge-base of the average business owner, including financial advisors and wealth managers. I include financial service entrepreneurs because they are technically trained in understanding how money works, but not all channels for revenue generation, high-volume sales, and customer acquisition costs. A shortcoming in these aspects leaves even an astute financial professional lacking finances to run their operation.

In many ways, the small business owner behaves similarly to the college student approached by the credit card company offering a free T-Shirt for their credit information. The focus on the gift and the excitement of the spending power of the credit card blinds the student from the responsibilities needed to manage the credit card. The credit card becomes an overly expensive lesson filled with regret due to a lack of knowledge or restraint. Owning a business carries the same connotation when the entrepreneur does not comprehensively weigh the factors of ownership and is seduced by time freedom, not being told what to do, and ideas of making a fortune. The lack of a formal opportunity costs analysis coupled with the absence of a process for conversion makes for a bad business decision. The entrepreneur's optimistic views are heavily embedded into the Expectancy Theory, leading a misguided train of thought producing false hope. This false hope steers away from success and brings regret.

CHAPTER 5

H_2O

Bruce Lee is arguably the most famous martial artist in history. He spoke about his martial art form, Jeet Kune Do, as being water. Water can take the form of any shape it occupies. Bruce Lee states,

> If you put water into a cup, it becomes the cup. You put water into a bottle, and it becomes the bottle. You put it in a teapot; it becomes the teapot. Now, water can flow, or it can crash. Be water, my friend.[1]

Bruce Lee used water as a metaphor to explain that flowing with a situation allows for understanding, leading to solutions to overcome it. One of the most effective methods of removing gum out of clothes is to use more gum. The sticky property of gum attracts the gum in the clothes and pulls it away from the garment. The same can be said for decision making in business and working with people. Adjusting to new circumstances or unfamiliar activities can be difficult, but the obvious answer is often overlooked for an external solution. Instead of acting as the force pressing against progression, operate as the current that flows to solutions.

Acting as the current to create solutions reduces stress and frustration in the lives of people and among business decisions. I witness people getting upset with others who do not agree with their perspective, causing more aggravation. Instead of acting as the solution, the person perpetuates the issue. Parents, teachers, spouses, and employers experience anxiety, anger, hopelessness, and stress because of differing perspectives and perceptions. This reality is common among business owners related to their products or services and the selected industry. A business owner's decision making is directly affected by the behavior of the target audience. Understanding the mentality of the intended audience sets the occasion for adjustment. Flowing as water speaks to the openness, willingness, and ability to pivot directions to progress the business.

Automotive Consulting

I held the position of Director of Sales for a large automotive franchise for seven years. The dealership was a staple of the city for 100 years with significant market share. Through my tenure, I increased the total number of sales, percentage of sales, and year over year sales every year. The volume and rate of sales were higher during this time than other periods over the previous 100 years. Since leaving the franchise, many of my original staff members are implementing the processes I taught. I left the automotive industry to create my global consulting firm, J.C. Baker & Associates—The Business Hospital. The original business plan was to travel around the United States to provide Leadership and Sales Training to car dealerships. The goal was to increase the productivity of these dealerships in the same manner as my previous franchise. I had a target list of 150 dealerships to solicit. I called my first two warm leads and cultivated a relationship to be hired by them. My previous dealership declined to hire me for my services, and so did the two warm leads after a month of intentional solicitation.

During that same period, tech startups began contacting me to assist with fundraising and pitch strategy. I took those opportunities, which led to new relationships in the tech space. Within two months, I was working on new product development for startups. Instead of fighting against the current, I flowed with the current and created a revenue stream from an international clientele base. The concepts and skills mastered over 20 years in corporate and sales transitioned into new business opportunities. The adjustment was a common-sense adaptation owing to the various positions I held throughout my life. The train of thought derived from using personal strengths to advance the career while placing a premium on enjoyable work.

I have not worked for a single automotive dealership since leaving the industry. However, I speak at national automotive conferences, and I have developed a proprietary automotive tool used to advance the industry. Both of these aspects originated from a conscious conversion from soliciting individual dealerships to providing value to the industry as a whole. One of the original warm leads disagreed with my offering quite passionately as my view of the industry is quite different from the traditional belief systems held by members in the industry. For example, concepts such as negotiating and working "bell to bell" (open to closing) for sales consultants are not a part of my training regimen. I promote shorter workdays and team selling methods, even with a commission compensation plan.

Despite my demonstrated success, the original warm lead challenged my position and questioned if I understood the car industry. Instead of experiencing irritation, considering my high recommendation by a mutual business partner to the warm lead, the focus shifted to impacting the entire industry. The meta-cognition exercise analyzed the known behaviors of every automotive General Manager I knew, coupled with historical practices. The thinking process led to the decision to work with companies actively seeking innovative strategy and imagination. The net effect resulted in a successful general consulting business practice allowing for diversity in ideation and innovation. Altering the execution plan from the automotive industry proved to be a good decision, but the decision came through recognizing opportunity, meta-cognition, and the historical train of thought of leveraging strengths. The decision to pivot from the automotive industry was not made in isolation based on a singular event. The openness and willingness to work with tech companies provided new opportunities to leverage.

Master a Niche

Flowing in any direction based on circumstance presents a counter issue with solidifying your value proposition and offers market confusion. Determining if you should transition your business or maintain your offering is a challenging dichotomy. Numerous options and dead ends are elements of distraction for business owners. Staying focused and perfecting the product or service may be the best option for the business owner. The trouble is how to know when to perform an action or not act. As the classic Kenny Rogers country song, The Gambler says, "You got to know when to hold em, know when to fold em, know when to walk away."[2] Determining the timing and the stimulus for change or ignoring distractions is a critical skill for decision making.

The primary determinant is the value proposition held by the business owner. If the business owner considers operating outside of the usual business framework causing an overhaul in operations and untested actions—keeping the current focus is the decision. If the transition highlights existing organizational or personal strengths, making the change could prove prudent. Even when companies try to shape multiple value propositions, they tend to align them only with a single customer value proposition, yet with little connection to their overall scaling objectives for the short-, mid-, and long-term. Thus, many companies do not scale because they were not initially designed to scale in the initial stages of their existence.[3] For instance, during the global COVID-19 pandemic, many companies turned their attention to personal protective equipment (PPE) because of the demand and the economic opportunity. I had clients that I advised against making the change to sell PPE owing to the organizational setup, human capital challenges, and lack of supply chain. To properly facilitate items such as facemasks, hand sanitizer, and forehead thermometers, the client would have needed to completely revamp their operation, invest in manufacturing, logistics, and a sales force. Although the opportunity to participate is a potentially lucrative return, the risk of failure also increases. Transitioning to PPE was not a direct scaling objective established from the beginning, operating as a benefit for all stakeholders. The unknown variables with transitioning poses more uncertainty than assurance. The operation will lean on trial and error as the PPE space is not a primary offering for them.

Conversely, another client of ours made a successful transition to the PPE space. This client has a 15-year history moving products nationwide with a fully integrated supply chain and commercial recognition. The client simply had to earmark space in their warehouse, change the SKUs, and inventory schedule to facilitate the change. The current operation had the bandwidth to double the production without adding new employees or altering their internal processes. Sourcing the PPE was a low-investment and a low-risk opportunity with the potential for high yields based on the structure of the operation. To scale company value rapidly, a company needs to develop value propositions for different parties, customers, investors, partners, suppliers, employees, and other resource owners, as well as align them with its scaling objectives.[3] This client benefited from openness and the willingness to offer different products based on the climate and demand in a manner that is conducive to the operation's structure. The decision traveled on the same train of thought as the company's initial foundation 15 years prior.

Action Is Faster than Reaction

My father is an expert martial artist as he is a fourth-degree Black Belt in three different styles. The styles he teaches are Ai Mute Shotokan, Modern Arnis, and Balintawak. There are two primary teachings he has impressed on me for decades. One concept is that action is faster than reaction, and the other is recognition, timing, and speed. These two concepts govern his beliefs on how to attack and defend. We have studied these concepts for years and integrated them into our personal and business practices. The train of thought is to generate activity before the competition to forcing them to react. Even a defensive move can force an offensive reaction. Recognition, timing, and speed refers to the ability to identify a stimulus and move accordingly, and therefore, you will appear faster than the opposition.

In a business sense, all of these aspects universally exist. A business owner benefits from taking action in the market dictating to the consumer base or the target audience. If the business owner reacts to the industry changes, capturing the market share could be lost. Recognizing the previous and current trends set the occasion for decisiveness, increasing the speed of the decision making and timing in the market. The business owner has to employ meta-cognition to execute the action and discern the stimulus appropriately. In other words, the owner must think about elements in the market ahead of time, prepare action steps, and outline signs that trigger movement. The analysis of the economic environment places a greater focus on how to execute new strategies for growth. Staying connected with the changes and analyzing the trends in business performance, analyzing performance indicators helps managers know not only their environment, the opponents, stakeholders, and the opportunities that can be optimized and used as advantages in a turbulent economic area.[4]

Conceptually and literally, business owners capitalize by starting trends, disrupting an industry, or overtaking a competitor as a new entrant. For instance, in times of disaster or crisis, many companies catapult their sales and grow their businesses. Investors are notorious for earning more dividends by contributing more during economic downturns and waiting for the economy to rebound. In many cases, investing during difficulty creates a positive turn. When others are waiting for the market to return, they lose higher yield spreads due to factors of demand and saturation. During the Coronavirus crisis, many tech companies benefited from the global shut down and quarantine protocols. The action of deploying technology to bring people together with the appropriate bandwidth and infrastructure serves as a headstart and a market controlling aspect above threats seeking to implement late. "The Theory of Economic Development," published in 1911 (itself a recessionary year), "the very logic of the capitalist system after some time of depression, new entrepreneurs would emerge and then there would be a new 'swarm' of entrepreneurs."[5] Employing the action steps into the train of thought places the expectation for adjustment and movement into the common-sense thought process.

Business owners need to outline the variables of adjustment in advance for a working consciousness when a change is necessary for sustainability.

Strategy variables:
- Risk versus opportunity
- Return on assets employed
- Turnover
- Market share
- Employee satisfaction
- Customer's expectation

Managerial variables:
- Resource availability
- Planning effort
- Cost income versus budget

Operational variables:
- Individual performance related to processes
- Corporate activities
- Products
- Procedures
- Efficiency measures

Adaptability and adjustments fall under the category of behavioral strategy allowing for new insights during strategic decision-making opportunities. The three variable types outlined previously highlight the needed tasks and activities for assessing change. Each component has an opportunity cost directly impacting the progress of the business. The discipline of utilizing a formal process to weigh the pros and cons of each variable pays dividends in knowledge and error reduction for the business owner. Diligence-based strategy offers an applied method for formulating and executing strategy in organizations, showing how managers can leverage resources to drive business success.[6] When a business owner applies a diligence-based strategy, analysis of the advantages is connected to the execution of basic principles. The basic principles serve as a guide for the business owner, and good and bad decisions derive from the ability to execute a given plan. In athletics, doing the fundamentals well provides any team with an opportunity to win. The concept of Walt Disney was to do the basics brilliantly. A diligence-based strategy gives a process for small business owners to stand on to govern their operation and make adjustments when necessary, led by brilliant basics.

A prudent business owner draws from all available information, indicators, and advice to build conclusions on how to navigate their business for the long term. Customer insights, market trends, consumer data, substitutes, complements, and emerging threats serve as indicators for a small business owner to decipher pivot decisions. Customer insights manifest in feedback, reviews, and surveys based on discovery and experience. Customer insights provide a valuable first-hand account of what to expect when changing a product or service. Market trends give a historical look at the direction and tendency of the market as a whole and the prevailing behaviors of the stakeholders. Consumer data provides information on potential customer attitudes and routines. Substitutes are other offerings that replace the business owner's primary offering. For instance, a vegan black-bean burger is a substitute for a traditional beef hamburger. Complements are business offerings that pair well with the business owner's primary offering. An example of a complement is the condiments of a burger, such as ketchup and mustard. Both of these products have a direct correlation with hamburger sales. Emerging threats are competitors seeking market share with the ability to pull consumers to their direction. All of these factors play an essential role when assessing opportunity costs and if a business owner should consider a pivot in operation. A formal design-led strategy extends thinking perspectives and should be adopted as a strategy-as-a-practice perspective.[7] The formal consideration of performance altering categories takes a calculated approach and plenty of skill-enhancing practice.

Practicing the skills of decision making surrounding opportunity costs include proactive organizational capabilities. All of the appointed leadership of a company must engage in actively initiating changes and participating in the development of future regulations for the benefit and influence of the stakeholders.[8] The proactive train of thought drives the focus further than the company's current status but works to understand how current decisions affect future business. The opportunity costs experienced at a later period are the reflection of decision-making processing in the present time. Demonstrating fluidity in operation takes a proactive mentality from the onset with the willingness to change course if the conditions are appropriate. Analyzing the conditions takes a diligence-based strategy and a structured decision-making approach.

The organizational environment has to foster an attitude of openness to influence the team members. In entrepreneurship and small business, the environment has been a significant contingency that moderates organizational size, technology, structure, resources, and capabilities on organizational performance.[9] Unlike the Expectancy Theory, a mentality of structure thinking, diligence-based strategy, and decision making increase the opportunity for success in all moderated areas of business. Small business owners benefit from leveraging the attitude of change when that change leverages the strengths of the operation, coupled with opportunity in the market. Careful and consistent deliberation of the organizational strategy reduces the remorseful effects of opportunity costs and places the owner in a position to take advantage of potential alterations in the business.

The organizational environment and tolerance are created by the attitude of the small business owner or entrepreneur. Entrepreneur types also determine the opportunity costs, consideration variables, and the train of thought. There are four categories of entrepreneurs that set the occasion for various decision-making scenarios.

1. Proactive entrepreneurs—are individuals internally motivated to pursue their own venture development on a full-time basis.
2. Reactive entrepreneurs—are individuals working full-time for their own business but are externally driven, that is, perceive no other viable option.
3. Dependent (part-time) entrepreneurs—are individuals who devote part-time effort to developing their own venture and are generally reliant on a supplemental source for income.
4. Corporate entrepreneurs—are individuals engaged in entrepreneurial activities in a firm where they are not the primary owners.[10]

The choices and alternatives considered are directly correlated with the level of ramification, risk, and reward at the given stage of the entrepreneur. Proactive entrepreneurs have more options to weigh during decision making than corporate entrepreneurs owing to the consequence's difference in responsibility and gravity—the corporate entrepreneur or (Intrapreneur) hedges decisions with the support and backing of the corporation. The result of the action may not determine their salary, benefits, or overall livelihood. The proactive entrepreneur has to generate revenue to not only succeed but also to survive financially. The pressure to perform is higher, even bringing a more significant burden to make better decisions. The train of thought for an entrepreneur to transition or alter their operation includes their current entrepreneurship status, the opportunity costs, and the effect on all stakeholders. Careful thought surrounding these aspects allow for a more fluid process and transition for the business owner.

Adjusting to the market or making changes in a company appropriately stem from a strong command of the operation and the confidence to execute critical components leading to success. Bruce Lee had confidence in altering his martial arts style because his train of thought set the course for his fighting style. Attributes such as speed, quickness, technique, and I.Q. were the foundation for his art. Those skills were transferable, allowing him to outmatch his opponents successfully. I was able to transition my target audience as a consulting firm because management consulting and organizational strategy were the primary elements of my service offering. I did not alter my operation to accommodate the shift in topic from the automotive industry to industry agnostic. Flowing like water represents maintaining your core value and shape-shifting to changes in your environment, allowing for sustainability and growth.

CHAPTER 6

Golden Rule

A common statement circulating among people regarding success is, "It is not what you know, but whom you know." This statement speaks about the perceived importance of developing a strong network of people and social currency. Building a pipeline of influencers, advocates, strategic partners, alliances, and team members is the single most critical element for sustainable business growth. There is an African Proverb that states, "If you want to go fast, go alone. If you want to go far, go together." This proverb speaks about the importance of teamwork and relationships. Building meaningful relationships or even valuable relationships takes time, energy, effort, and careful attention. Relationships are the building blocks of good business decision making and ultimately determine if a deal is made, a project is completed, or an innovative advancement is realized. How to engage and treat people appropriately is not a common-sense skill and is widely taken for granted.

All relationships are not equal or equitable. Treating people the same is a noteworthy goal but a misplaced practice in reality. Personal relationships, family relationships, romantic relationships, and business relationships vary in purpose and structure. My relationship with my wife differs significantly from my three daughters, although they are a part of my family relationship group. My three daughters have a five-year and an eight-year gap between them, respectively. My relationship with them is very different due to their age and life stages, even though they are all my daughters within the family group.

In business, the relationship with the senior practitioners of my company varies from that of the junior practitioners. The relationship with my practitioners differs from my relationship with my clients, even in the business relationship sector. The notion that we can attain equal treatment of all relationships creates unrealistic expectations and frustration in relationship maintenance. The goal is to nurture relationships to maximize the potentiality of every connection. Concepts such as respect, trust, loyalty, and liking hold prominent roles in how people perceive their relationships.

Treating others with respect is a personal and business decision connected with healthy relationships. The train of thought to properly execute respecting others falls in line with meta-cognition. Actively thinking of the ways your behavior affects others, and they perceive those behaviors is a level of effort and energy that people may not be willing to give. To respect others and provide suitable treatment to others has to be explicitly defined. The person also has to be prepared to produce the necessary action to execute the described aspects. The Golden Rule is ethical conduct stemming from the Bible passages Matthew 7:12 and Luke 6:31, which translates as, "Do to others as you would have them do to you."[1] This ethical principle is a standard reference and widely believed. In Judaism, the Talmud states, "What is hateful to you, do not do to your fellowman. That is the entire law, all the rest is commentary."[2] Confucianism states, "Surely it is the maxim of loving-kindness: Do not unto others that you would not have them do unto you."[3] In Islamic doctrine, it is written, "No one of you is a believer until he desires for his brother what he desires for himself."[4] The passages illustrate the priority in treating others like yourself as a demonstration of respect.

Individual Respect

A general acceptance is that we should treat people the way that "we" like to be treated as a baseline for respect and consideration. The emphasis is treating people in the manner that "you" would treat "yourself," which is an internal reflective process. It is implied that people treat themselves well, serving as the baseline for appropriate interaction. I will offer an additional viewpoint to the Golden Rule perspective through experience. Many people do not treat themselves well, respect themselves, or take thought on how their decisions affect them. How someone treats themself is not indicative of how I would like to be treated. The higher thought of treatment is analyzing how a person wants to be treated and behave accordingly. This train of thought is an external cognitive process.

Emotions about a situation are commonly used as a barometer of how to interact with someone. We cannot lean on how we feel or a personal perspective to serve as a precursor to how to treat someone because of the innate differences in people. I am not in disagreement with the religious text mentioned previously; I am taking the principles one level higher to achieve a greater understanding and execution within relationships. It is acceptable for one person to refer to them on a first-name basis in business, but the other person may prefer a formal title in a professional setting. To operate under the assumption that the other person accepts a first-name acknowledgment could be viewed as a sign of disrespect. This form of disrespect can damage the business relationship rendering the decision to refer to the person by the first name as a bad decision. Using the first name may not be an active decision but a muscle memory behavior connected to the common-sense practice in other settings. Hence the reason why relationship building can be a never-ending and challenging task. It is uncommon in people's minds to view a reference to a name as a business decision. Relational aspects can vary and may not connect from setting to setting. Some business relationships are established on a golf-course, boardroom, social gathering, or direct solicitation. Each of these relationships will manifest separate realities for what is expected or determined as the "norm." The appropriate step is learning more about the characteristics of the person you are building the relationship with and work to execute the expectations.

Leadership Style

Every business owner needs to discover and learn their business style. Knowing your style lets you articulate your style to the business stakeholders, minimizing errors in operation. In business relationships, it is difficult to engage effectively if the people closest to you are unsure of your leadership style and even more if they are uncertain of the leadership they prefer. There are plenty of leadership styles employed by business owners. Leadership styles include but are not limited to:

1. Shared leadership—All decision makers distribute leadership responsibilities equally.

2. Democratic—All members of the organizations are encouraged to share opinions through the appointed leader.

3. Laissez-Faire—Absence of leadership.

4. Transactional—Performance-based through a system of rewards and consequences.

5. Autocratic—Unilateral decision making.

6. Transformational—The four constructs.
    (a) Inspired Motivation
    (b) Idealized Influence
    (c) Individual Consideration
    (d) Intellectual Stimulation[5]

Each leadership style carries a benefit based on the audience and the nature of the relationship. A shared leadership style may work more appropriately in a room of high-level executives combining skillsets under a joint-venture agreement. It is reasonable to conclude that a top-tier CEO working with another accomplished CEO would appreciate information sharing and decision agreement. In the military, ranking officers have to be granted and submitted to autocratic leadership. In moments of great crisis, choices may need to be swift and decisive. This scenario does not lend to a shared leadership model. With a sales force, transactional and laissez-faire leadership are typical models. Salespeople tend to work under a commissioned or incentive-based pay plan programming the staff to perform for recognition, bonuses, or job security. Transactional leadership works in these environments and are usually controlled by the changing of awards or competition. Laissez-faire works in the same situations when tenured sales consultants exist. Often, senior sales staff members appreciate autonomy and the freedom to exercise decisions.

Transformational leadership works in all situations owing to the general structure of the four constructs. The third construct of Individual Consideration speaks about the need to view people independently and learn how to better work with them. The train of thought is to understand the needs and wants of the people to offer more value to the relationship. In business-to-business (B2B) settings, the relationship between the parties involved is one of the most critical elements contributing to success. In this context, a relationship can be considered to be an ongoing exchange of resources between two or more parties where there is some expectation that these exchanges will continue in the future.[6] Individual Consideration enhances the exchange between two members. A good business person uses the relationship information for mutual benefit. The longer the transfer of value, the longer the relationship lasts. Relationship building uses contextual clues that are observed through close and intentional engagement. The train of thought reflects the fundamentals of the Golden Rule because if the goal is to treat others as you would like to be treated, then deliberately learning the interests of others satisfies the rule.

I was a top sales professional for a national pharmaceutical company promoting a pain portfolio. Having access to speak to the physicians is a difficult task when combining the multiple layers of gatekeepers, the busy work schedule, patient needs, and competition. The key to earning face time with the doctors was treating the gatekeepers the way they wanted to be treated. Each hospital, medical facility, and private practice had a separate method for entry and access. One facility might require a signature in a logbook, another might require sampling for a while, and another might instruct you to schedule a time. These steps were mere formalities and but not the essential elements. Relationships with the gatekeepers determined the amount of time you had with a physician, if the doctor saw your product, favor above the competition, and product recommendation to a patient. These realities were heightened by relationship building through Individual Consideration. Bringing food, remembering a birthday, acknowledging a new hairstyle, or asking about a family member served as business decisions. By asking about the "likes" of the gatekeepers, it allowed them to articulate how they want to be treated.

The process of asking what others wanted or how they liked to be treated became a staple of my sales operation. The common-sense aspect of my train of thought is that it is reasonable to believe that others appreciate the gesture of learning their interest instead of assuming their interest. For instance, if I bring donuts to a medical office and the members appreciate the gift, assuming that the next office wants those same donuts is an error. The following office may wish to have a healthier snack alternative. Donuts will not impact the office the same as there is no value in the sugary snack item. The same action serving as a good business decision can manifest as a bad business decision with a separate office.

Power Exertion

Building relationships and teams are a delicate process with many theories on the best method to accomplish either task. Treating people with respect and individual consideration are components of best practices. Another element in relationships is the concept of power. The definition of power by social psychologist J. P. French and Bertram Raven in 1959 states that power is "the ability to manage the other party's perceptions."[7] Managing the perceptions of others derives from asking people how they like to be treated and recognizing the existing formal power. In business, there are always power constructs in relationships. The customer may hold a particular influence over the business owner. The business owner may have a specific power over an employee. Learning the different power types provides structure to the train of thought and enhances the common-sense thinking when engaging with people. The original five formal powers as coined by Bertram Raven are:

1. Coercive power—Driven by fear of consequence.
2. Reward power—Driven by benefit or compensation.
3. Legitimate power—Appointed leadership or title.
4. Expert power—Driven by expertise or credential.
5. Referent power—Driven by respect and ability.[6]

How these separate powers are recognized and used in relationships determines how people react and respond to the dynamics of the relationship. An appointed leader can confuse the business title as an opportunity to exert coercive power over a workforce that is familiar with a referent power culture. Only leaning on the subjective view of power sets the occasion for misconceptions and rebellion. This reality would serve as a bad decision for the newly appointed leader and the stakeholders. Conversely, if an appointed leader seeks to operate by reward power and the members expect expert power, then a mismatch of confidence can occur.

The concept of Individual Consideration does not imply the loss of personal identity, but to be mindful of the target audience you are seeking to build the relationship. It is not common to formally discuss power constructs in the business realm as the concepts are more psychological and

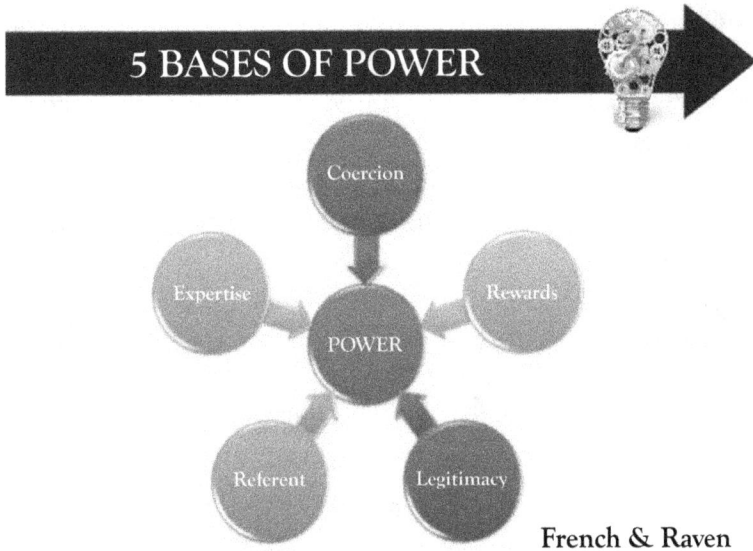

Figure 6.1 The five bases of power[8]

academic. However, business owners benefit from understanding how their power exertion fits their engagement activity.

Not only does the power exertion of a relationship exist as a business decision, but so does the personal connectivity of salespeople and customers. The change of a salesperson can have a profound effect on business, especially among B2B relationships. Many people believe changing sales personnel may serve as an adverse action, but there is evidence that a change can bring success to a company. Using multilevel loyalty theory and relationship life cycle theory, the authors offer a comprehensive conceptualization of potentially countervailing consequences of relationship disruptions. In particular, disruptions may have different effects on resale revenue versus new sale revenue, contingent on both the history and expected future development of the relationship.[9] The rationale posits that relationship development or change reflects the expectation or need of the consumer base. Adding a new salesperson to an account can exert excitement and energy into a product or a service, which may be a request of the customer.

At other times, changing salespeople may reduce revenue owing to the comfort and affinity between the salesperson and the customer. Relationship management is a critical factor in decision making, especially when considering a business shift or pivot. The opportunity cost of making the change has to include all of the current and future developed relationships to ensure the appropriate engagement for sustainability. Evaluating the relationships among all stakeholders pre- and postchange is a prudent exercise and needs to be programmed into the train of thought for owners. Ignoring the impact of relationship management is dangerous and risky for a business owner of any size business.

Connected to relationship management is the component of trust in business relationships. The elevated view of the Golden Rule points to relationship building through treating people how they would like to be treated. A residual of this treatment is a buildup of trust between members in the relationship. Trust is one of three components commonly spoken of in research regarding successful business relationships. Trust, power, and money are viewed as coordination mechanisms channeling people's expectations and triggering specific patterns of interaction.[10] The trust of a business partner, consumer, or strategic alliance can be severed by distrust, power struggles, and money issues.

Taking the appropriate time to nurture relationships with these three aspects in mind minimizes relational risk. Small business owners and entrepreneurs have to leverage connections for sustainability. Errors in relationship management cripple small business owners, especially startup founders or microbusiness owners. In some cases, a boutique or microbusiness owner may have one large client and a few small clients sustaining their business. To lose the business from the significant partner serves as a crippling action for the business owner. The relationship becomes vital to the business owner, and therefore, consideration of the client's treatment is a premium. Understanding and operating according to the client's wishes and interests becomes the most crucial decision of the business owner. A good comprehension of the power construct and trust-building bodes well for longevity for the business owner. A healthy balance of trust and power mitigates the effect of the trade-offs in relationship management, allowing for a better appreciation of value among both parties.[11] It is incumbent on the business owner to uphold the balance of the relationship and uncover ways to demonstrate value based on the consumer's articulated views, strategic alliance, or client. Business aspects such as contracts, prices, coordination of activities, sensemaking, and information sharing extend from the notion of trust and power.[12] Managing the relationships with particular concern reduces or even eliminates business aspects in the future among stakeholders. Learning how people like to be treated in this scenario bodes well for the business and manifests as a good decision making for the short- and the long-term.

Implementing the skillset of relationship management in the train of thought provides dividends through business relationships and human capital. Aspects such as networking, sales, business development, leadership, training, and governance are made better when employing the Golden Rule. The practice of the enhanced version of the Golden Rule yields a positive return in all relationships, from personal to business. The interdependence of relationships calls for a strong command of relationship management and soft people skills, which are often neglected or minimized. Treating others the way that they would like to be treated takes patience and active listening. These two attributes serve as good business decision-making skills for longevity and sustainability.

CHAPTER 7

Mine or Yours

Commonly, the boundaries of ownership are misconstrued and violated. The challenge in this chapter is to reflect on common thoughts surrounding ownership, governance, and responsibility. Overall, our general society reinforces our learning about ownership with misleading symbols. Our views on dating relationships, possession of objects, and rights protection are misguided from adolescence to adulthood. My children make declarations of ownership throughout the house, claiming their toys, rooms, snacks, and privacy. My rebuttal is always direct and transparent regarding their lack of ownership but stewardship. In dating relationships, it is common for people to refer to their love interest as "my man" or "my woman." There is a label of mental ownership and possessiveness embedded in the connotation. All the psychological and emotional connectivity exists without going through the appropriate process to establish ownership. This behavior exists in the business realm also—premature claims to business concepts, deals, and even the business structure.

Stewardship is the supervision, care, or management of something. People will confuse their responsibility of stewardship appointed by someone else, like ownership. Mental ownership of a project, job, or process is important for any task or goal's success. The mental ownership allows a person to perform their duties better due to the connectivity of the work. However, mental ownership and stewardship are not the same as formal ownership. The boundaries and lines of stewardship and ownership get confused and misguided, leading toward bad decisions.

Ownership

Ownership takes place in two methods, mental ownership and formal ownership. My daughters take psychological ownership over their bedrooms and material items. They make it known when they say, "Get out of my room" or "Give me back my toy." The lesson is that nothing is technically owned until you sign a contract for it or purchase it. The appropriate documentation signifies car ownership. Volumes of documentation recognize homeownership. Accepting the responsibility for a natural or adopted child is associated with paperwork while signatures and licenses acknowledge marriages. Legal filings identify business ownership. The train of thought for good business decision making is formalizing your company's structure and signing for the asset. The parameters of ownership are clearly outlined when executed through the allotted process. Tax ramifications, human capital needs, and strategic partnerships align better with a formally structured business.

Business ownership has many forms in today's business climate. Social media has empowered a new generation of business owners, and the guidelines of a business owner have stretched to unrecognizable aspects. Business ownership includes large corporations to home-based Internet businesses to freelance gigs. This more open version of business is conducive for new entrepreneurs and revenue channels for even working-class people. One downside to the many options to business ownership is the possibility of poorly formed businesses. A startup company may file for intellectual property protection and neglect to legally establish the appropriate company structure. A contracted worker may operate as a sole proprietor without any legal protection while providing services. A nonprofit director may work on the organization's mission without formally existing as a recognized 510c3 public charity. The highlighted examples are real-world examples of people expressing ownership to their target audience without solidifying legitimate ownership. Each of these scenarios has a form of ownership but lacks completion leaving the person with additional exposure and risk.

A company's legal status can be a sole proprietorship, partnership, or corporation. Selecting the appropriate company structure can be done without the guidance of legal representation, but the filing individual assumes the risk in that case. As the owner of The Business Hospital, I work daily with new and established business owners. One of the milestones I cover during the business physical is my proprietary 22 Step Checklist™. The 22 Step Checklist™ is a business audit serving as a due diligence process for the company. One of the steps is to confirm the company's filing status if they are a prerevenue or newly established company without a tax filing. I find through my assessments that many of my clients have incomplete or nonexistent filings. Our Legal Wing assists them with their set up, ensuring proper ownership. I uncover unexecuted partnerships, corporations without the appropriate documentation, and nonprofit organizations without formal board members.

Completing the company structure is an action faster than reaction step for the potential business owner. Working with legal representation to create the company serves as a good decision to widen the parameters and scope of legal understanding. If a company has partners or is a joint venture, then the shares, corporate expectations, and policies become an immediate priority. Conversations on equity, internal controls, severability, exits, incentives, and governance are of high legal importance. These factors are not the only factors, but outlining a precise detail of what ownership means in the formal structure's confines, sets the occasion for good decision making. Without sound documentation and the appropriate filings, many people believed they owned businesses only to realize they were not protected as an owner financially or legally. Issues such as the proper number of shares or equity per owner can become a point of contention when the terms are not clearly described. For example, when the number of owners increases, the shares for each partner decrease, the need for information sharing increases, and the risk for misconception and impropriety increases.[1] The need for formal guidelines filed during the formulation protects the integrity and the longevity of the company. The business owner would have accomplished the first task as a business owner, establishing the company's foundation.

Family businesses, microbusinesses, and large companies differ significantly in a myriad of categories. Employee count, office size, and consumer reach are a few of the ways these businesses differ. One misnomer that I see regularly is that smaller businesses do not have to prepare in the manner of larger companies. This train of thought leads to omissions in detail, opening the company to unnecessary risk. A sole proprietor will file as a Limited Liability Company (LLC) without completing an operating agreement and setting up payroll. These two examples are simple actions for a business, but they do not exist in the common-sense sphere for entrepreneurs. Missing or ignoring details in formal structure tends to lead to additional omissions as well. The omissions transform into hidden practices, shaped by the dynamics of the business operator. While their business activities are legal, the governance and ownership structures of their organizations are illegal, inadequate, or nonexistent.[2] Informal entrepreneurship exists due to a lack of knowledge and attention to detail in company creation. This behavior is bad decision making and serves as the potential for future bad decisions.

A family-owned business may not exemplify the same capital needs as a large corporation, but the quality of the contractual structure needs to be as strong.[3] Formal clauses to safeguard the family ownership, control, and financial independence hinges on the initial setup and attitude toward the business creation. The business owner's meta-cognitive activity is to solidify all of the steps to ensure the protection and provision of legal ownership. I have worked with clients seeking to remove a member of the business, change the pay structure, or plan to sell portions of the business to another entity but run into roadblocks due to company structural error. The business "owner" sets the course to enforce a dissolution to find out that they do not have the appropriate power to remove the other party due to absent or incomplete documentation. Funding potential and investment opportunities are not realized because of inadequate paperwork and the lack of diligence on behalf of the business owner.

During the COVID-19 pandemic crisis, the United States government offered Federal programs to stimulate the economy by assisting small business owners through the EIDL (Economic Injury Disaster Loan) and the PPP (Paycheck Protection Program). Many small business owners claimed the need for these funds, and the proof of operational compliance and stability was not mandated to display from the onset. Many business owners simply had to answer a few questions without a scrutinized due diligence process to prove their position as a company. The reporting of documentation was a future requirement creating a return in pay and financial penalty scenario for informal entrepreneurs or business owners with poor structure. This reality is an example of a bad structure decision leading to future bad business decisions.

The company's business model is a key determinant of the formal business structure. The business model reflects the company's value proposition and articulates the offering to the target audience. How the business owner chooses to engage with the consumer also determines the precise structuring needs. For instance, a company with a philanthropic mission may choose to operate as a nonprofit organization or a for-profit company with a Corporate Social Responsibility (CSR) to accomplish the same mission. The decision derives from the product or service offered to the public and the revenue channels and distribution model. A company's business model has been argued to be the essential factor in its success or failure in the marketplace—more so than other factors. With more strategy research, the business model has been seen as an operative plan and a helpful visualization of the organization to support decision making in organizational management.[4] If a business intends to build from daily microtransactions, large deal-making, real estate venturing, employee-based operations, contractor-led activities, or a service-based solution, the model, represents the interaction between the strategy, connectivity, and execution. The ownership structure has to reflect the business model's position to reduce the risk profile of the business and maximize operational efficiency. If a business owner sets up the company structure to utilize 1,099 contract workers, then the resources and assets used in conjunction with the resources from the contractor must be formally outlined. In other words, the ownership of equipment, products, intellectual property, and other assets must be formally articulated and agreed on to avoid future conflict and confusion.

Family-run businesses suffer from blurred lines and inconsistency in structure because of the family connection and affinity. There are many reasons for the improper structure of a family business, including relationship management, succession management, remuneration for family members, and improper contractual agreements.[5] A forward-thinking process of outlining roles, responsibilities, authority, workflow, company structure, pay plans, and legal obligations eliminate future issues. Every aspect of the business should have a formalized control outlining and determining the ownership breakdown, and the expectations associated with the ownership.

I served a client with a complex family-owned business dynamic as the ownership consisted of parents, siblings, and spouses. There were a total of 10 owners with varying engagement in the business. The primary owner was the sole revenue generator and was also the primary financial investor. Another sibling was considered secondary because of their knowledge of the industry. One of the siblings was a silent participant, did not make a financial investment into the company, and was granted ownership because of her sibling status. Other members worked in the company inconsistently, and they did not have formal responsibilities within the company. This informal and incomplete operational structure was problematic for decision making on deals, purchases, and operational matters. The scenario became more complicated when one of the siblings decided to leave the company, and the equity from the departure had to be distributed. The other family members fought over the equity left by the sibling, but they did not want the additional company debt associated with the departure. After conducting a Business Physical™, I uncovered that none of the agreements had been formalized, documented, or filed, including the original structure of the company. The family members learned that they were an informal entrepreneurship group with no strong claims to any of the business assets. The assets of the business were not legally bound, creating more problems for the family. Ignoring a formal structuring process to ensure ownership is the most prime example of bad business decision making.

Many people view the goal of ownership as possession of something for longevity or to control the actions of the owned possession. Achieving sustainability takes a conscious effort to formalize appropriately, understand the dynamics of ownership, and have protection plans for the assets. This concept is true among all types of ownership, including property, vehicles, financial instruments, business, or anything of value. When applying this thought to vehicles, a buyer must purchase a vehicle through binding contractual paperwork establishing ownership, understand if the vehicle is "As-Is," has an extended service agreement, gap protection, and the overall terms of the financing and lastly purchase insurance in the event of a collision or total loss. Buying a vehicle is a formalized process with checks and balances to ensure the life cycle of ownership.

The organizational life cycle of a company is the same. The life cycle is a crucial element for the sustainability of the business. The initial stage in the life cycle of a business is the formalization of the company. The structure determines the roles, responsibilities, rewards, and risks. The growth portion of the cycle is an evolutionary stage defined through a sequence of stages that moves the company from a startup to a mature and larger company with the theme of ensuring the efficiency and continuity of the business.[6] Defining aspects such as the power structure, commitment levels, mission, vision, value proposition, and workflow process are vital for universal buy-in and execution. The business needs protection by way of insurance, formalized internal controls, risk assessments, and documentation. The owner is responsible for each stage of the provision securing a healthy future for the operation. Each step proves as prudent and good decision making.

Governance

Governance is an essential aspect for large publicly traded companies as well as entrepreneurs. Corporate governance carries the image of ownership owing to the high level of responsibility and control over a business entity. Establishing governance is a process set on guiding principles to regulate corporate action. Formal governance structures are helpful with aspects including capital markets, innovation, overall growth, corporate strategy, and the financial activity of a company. The decision-making power is appointed to the members operating as the formal corporate governance team. The shareholders or appointed board of directors are charged with maintaining the long-term success of the company. The members have to sign agreements for their position and are held liable for their actions in their role. Transparency in corporate governance is essential for the growth, profitability, and stability of any business.[7] Sound corporate governance is a useful and necessary element for businesses of all sizes and classes. Corporate governance is mainly achieved by introducing controlling bodies and formal structures such as councils and boards with clear power structures to avoid future conflicts.[6]

Examples of CEOs losing their role within their company are prevalent and visible. When a CEO is voted out or removed from a company, these decisions are made and executed by the corporate governance members. The demonstrated control gives the appearance of ownership in the company. In some cases, the corporate governance members are shareholders representing the financial ownership stake in the company. This combination of duality creates confusion for the novice business owner when contemplating a corporate governance structure for their boutique business. As such, the notion that shareholders, directors, and executives are the three primary forces responsible for determining corporate direction and action, they work in tandem with the CEO, owners, and top management teams.[8] The micro- or boutique business owner can benefit from having a small board of executives assisting with the business' governance, even if they do not have termination power. The roles and responsibilities are expressed directly in writing. The train of thought is to outline as much of the operation as possible to reduce confusion and minimize sustainability errors.

The growing role of corporate governance is growing among all sectors and business sizes. The meta-cognitive aspect derives from assembling others with the expertise, connectivity, and values of the company to demand better controls for accountability. When considering the decision-making process, business owners benefit from additional perspectives and a known system for checks and balances. Increased accountability ensures the integrity of the operation from financial reporting, daily tasks, reputation management, and goal attainment. Smaller companies benefit by adding value to the development strategy, while larger companies protect the interest of absent shareholders.[9] Leveraging a good corporate governance structure emphasizes the prudence and wisdom of the business owner. These are some of the aspects business owners obtain oversight through corporate governance:

1. Prepare and publish the mission statement of enterprises.
2. An enterprise policy statement to manage business growth.
3. Enterprise successions plan.
4. Annual management and accomplishment statements.
5. Management structure and level of professional qualification relevant to the industry.
6. Method of accounting and disclosure of audited account.
7. Stakeholder relations and welfare undertook by the enterprise.
8. Legal and regulatory compliance.[9]

As important as these items are to a large company for compliance and public opinion, an entrepreneur benefits from this guidance even more. A sole proprietor carries the responsibilities of every function of the business.

There are many instances where the entrepreneur is not classically trained in an area of business or is not adept in a division. The corporate governance provides strength in the areas lacking without adding the expense of additional employees. Creating a board of advisers, directors, or governors is a common-sense approach to action is faster than reaction. The business owner has the opportunity to develop the written policy that the board uses to govern it. The business owner demonstrates control over future decisions by initiating the decision to implement corporate governance.

As a solo entrepreneur, steps such as formalizing a board of advisers may appear unnecessary, but to the contrary, the formal governance assists with blind-spots and objective positions that the entrepreneur is incapable of viewing. A formal board serves as a team for the entrepreneur, even if they do not have decision-making power or job execution duties. Talking through issues, ideating on concepts, and discussing strategy from a dedicated board serves as a consistent method for good decision making.

Types of Commitment

There are many instances where commitment is interpreted as genuine involvement or mental ownership. Partnerships and joint ventures dissolve quickly and appear before arbitrators or judges owing to the misdiagnosis of commitment. Poor interpretation or communication of commitment also convinces business owners to enter incomplete agreements leading to additional risk. As in any other aspect of a business, all agreements must be formally constructed and appropriately filed. Agreeing on the commitment levels must be acknowledged and defined for the benefit of the involved parties.

There are three types of commitment levels that business owners must know.

1. Affective—Emotional attachment, affinity, and internal desire.
2. Continuance—Need-based and fear of loss.
3. Normative—Obligation and expected.

The types of commitment are essential to recognize in an ownership position. When selecting board members, partners, strategic alliances, and employees, understanding and articulating the expected commitment sets the foundation. Organizational commitment is the extent of an individual's loyalty to the company. A common barrier is an owner who believes that the commitment levels between partners and joint ventures are identical merely because they are participating in the company's development. The hope for any business owner is that Affective Commitment is the driving force behind the participation. Formal structuring and the appropriate documentation will ensure Normative Commitment or Continuance Commitment to the company's benefit. Without the proper documentation, individuals can find themselves faced with debts and liabilities from a failed partnership or joint venture. Litigation can extend from a hearsay defense of mine versus yours in the court of law over significant financial obligations.

Supported

Value Alignment

Affective Commitment

Valued

Fairly Treated

Figure 7.1 Affective commitment[10]

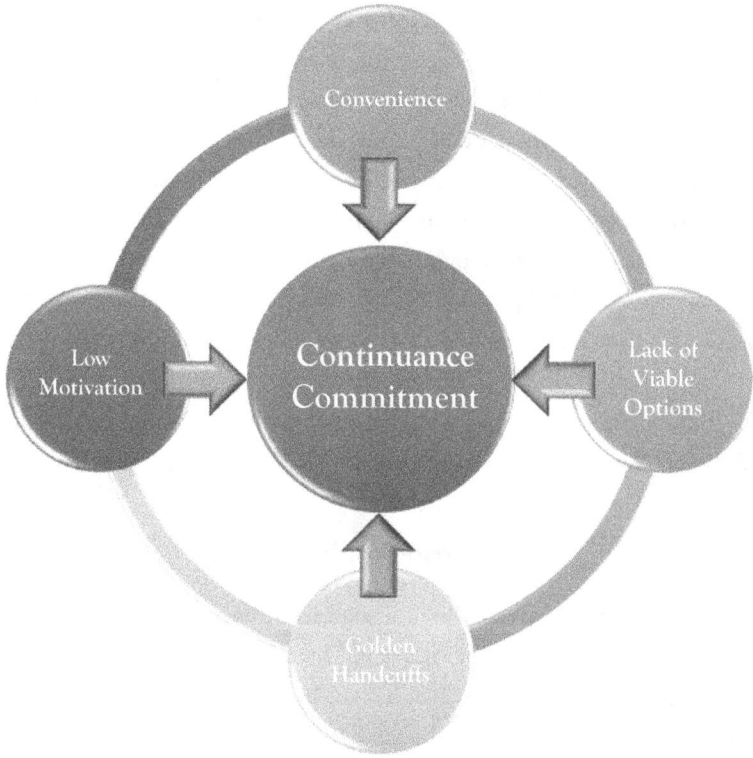

Figure 7.2 Continuance commitment[10]

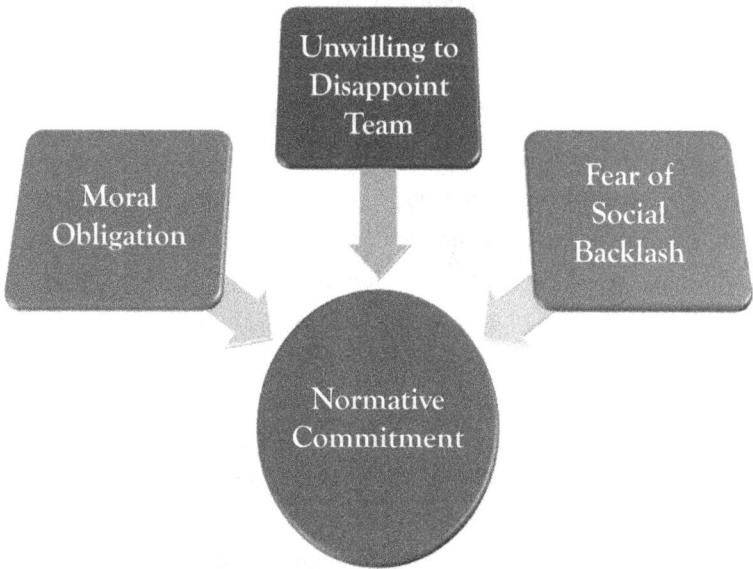

Figure 7.3 Normative commitment[10]

Organizational commitment is key in determining mental ownership in a company or a position. Formal conversations among partners and employees, assist with clarity in operation and execution. Not defining the commitment sets the occasion for assumptions in connectivity and execution. One common issue I see in my work are issues among business partners with separate ideas on engagement and undertaking. One member believes they have ownership over various aspects or assets of a business because they have an Affective Commitment to the business. The formal owner makes decisions contrary to affectively committed partner or family member, and legal disagreements arise. Conducting meaningful and difficult conversations from the onset of the business relationship minimizes the opportunity for explosive and divisive outcomes.

Scenario Application

A client of mine (Partner 1) built a successful business with his brother (Partner 2) in the social service space. The organization performed services with the youth sector, which has the passion of both partners. After a few years of successful growth, the partners questioned the long-term ramifications of the growth and who benefited most. Arguments and disagreements became the normal behavior between the partners. I was hired to assist with the company valuation and negotiations to sever the business relationship equitably. After conducting a Business Physical™, I learned that Partner 1 was responsible for the bulk of the annualized growth and market share in the region but did not have formal agreements for his role and function with the business. Partner 2 was responsible for the documentation and the initial investments. Although Partner 1 was the driver of the vehicle, he placed himself at a disadvantage due to the lack of formal structuring during business formulation. Partner 1 displayed Affective Commitment to the company while Partner 2 displayed Normative Commitment. However, the formal structure and positioning of Partner 2 allowed him to benefit during negotiations.

Scenarios such as this one reflects the question of "Mine or Yours" in business. Financially, a person buys a house and states that the house is "theirs." If they purchase the home through the financing from a bank, the bank then reflects their interest in the home through a lien position.

If the homeowner does not make the payments per the formal agreement with the bank, then the bank can seize it, essentially taking ownership. This aspect leads to the question, who does the house really belong to? The answer is, the house is the property of the owner who signed the documentation (Title, Declarations, etc.) but carries another set of guidelines owing to the financial documentation binding to the bank. The bank collateralizes the home to ensure they will receive their payment. As long as the homeowner makes the payments and eventually pays the financial debt, they own the house. The primary aspect to understand in this scenario is that the arrangement is formally drawn from the beginning outlining all the expectations, responsibilities, penalties, and processes for engagement. Small business owners benefit from a formalized process at the beginning of their business venturing. Carefully and attentively outlining the ownership guidelines and governance for any size company serves as good decision making.

CHAPTER 8

Interdependence

Entrepreneurs have many motivational factors leading to their actions to start a business. Their unique talents, career success, or longing to act independently of others are few inspirational reasons. What business owners soon find out is that all their actions and decisions depend on other factors and require a high level of interdependence with other elements. It is common for people to believe that their efforts are individualized and primarily have a personal effect. An inclusive paradigm leads to increased understanding and overall success. The train of thought is having an appreciation of how all things work together as necessary factors for business growth and sustainability. The act of meta-cognition works directly with the recognition, timing, and speed of an individual's action. The action of the owner affects future decisions, which produces new outcomes for scrutiny. Understanding how all the relationships, decisions, activities, and behaviors connect provides greater insight for the business owner.

Interdependence is the dependence of two or more aspects on each other. In relationships, interdependence is the degree to which people are mutually dependent on the others, while dependent relationships have an imbalance of dependency. Some of the people are reliant, and others are not. The lack of proportion represented creates lower value and resentment. Many entrepreneurs feel this emotion working in companies where the dependency appears or is uneven. Employees may believe that their company needs them more than they need the job. Many companies articulate that they are more valuable than the staff deeming them expendable. Successful operations recognize that all parties are interdependent and need each other to survive.

The ecosystem of nature is an excellent example of interdependence. Every participant in the environment benefits from the existence of each other. The producers and consumers in the food chain have an essential function in balancing life and creating sustainability. The elements of the

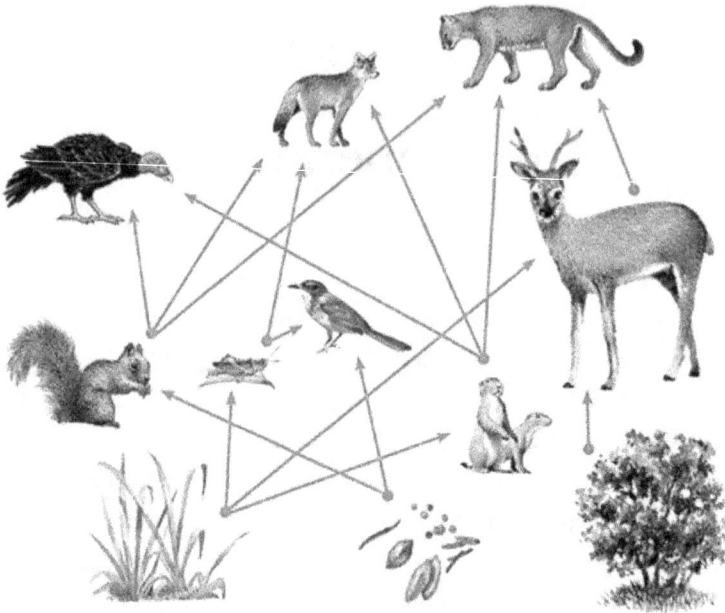

Figure 8.1 Why plants and animals are interdependent[1]

Earth, such as the Sun and rain, contribute to the ecosystem providing necessary attributes to sustain life.

Business owners benefit by understanding this same concept of business interdependence. The acknowledgment of interdependence allows for a strategy to leverage all the connecting components intentionally. Large multinational companies have utilized this principle for their economic gain. These companies realized the advantage and encourage cross-unit collaboration in the realm of strategic planning, budgeting, project management, shared services, and even centralized portfolio management.[2] Each aspect of a business named carries a level of crossover to the other portion of the company. A decision made in one realm has a profound impact on the other domains. Recognizing interdependence reduces the number of emotional or spontaneous choices and sets the framework for more calculated decision making. The meta-cognitive aspect earmarks focus on the ancillary portions of the business and allow for variables in those sections. In other words, the business owner thinks of all the potential connections to major decisions to hedge the corporate risk.

In a real-world example, my company J.C. Baker & Associates - The Business Hospital dissolved a joint venture due to the lack of appreciation of the interdependence created within our manufacturing wing. A partner company decided to violate the information-sharing clauses set out in our operating agreements. Our corporate governance sent an internal document revising and reminding the internal controls for compliance. The joint venture partner believed their role in the business operations was independent of the entire organization. The joint venture partner's role was business development and deal making. My company was responsible for the supply chain, liability, and the overall execution of the operation. As the revenue increased, the joint venture partner believed their business development effort was more valuable than the supply chain. The corporate governance detected impropriety, and my company was able to act swiftly based on the soundness of the information and common-sense positioning created by meta-cognition. As an experienced executive, the decision-making process and the action steps to dissolve was clean and straightforward. History coupled with recognition, timing, and speed produced the action is faster than reaction element. J.C. Baker & Associates did not lose any assets, relationships, deals, or revenue through the dissolution process. The process took roughly a week to conclude without significant disruption to operations. The fallacy in the joint venture partner's thought process is that the interdependence factor was undervalued as they were self-absorbed in their duties and not the larger picture for future sustainability.

The concept of interdependence should be clear in theory because we live our daily life under the constructs of interdependence. We carry the burden of providing for ourselves and the welfare of the family, friends, and our community. This burden happens through raising a family, paying taxes, or helping a friend. Some people believe that leaning on others is a symbol of weakness or inadequacy. Many common quotes are perpetuating this line of thinking. Statements such as, "When you want to do a job right, do it yourself," "Don't lean on others, you were born with two feet for a reason," and "God helps those who help themself" mislead people into feeling insufficient when running a company. The paradigm of interdependence has to change for overall business growth.

1. Interdependence is a higher value than independence. The fact that people are interdependent in relations allows people to do what works best for both parties.
2. Conscious interdependence initiates sincere and reliable agreements based on the mutual needs of each other.
3. Personal growth and maturity are of paramount importance to remain secure in your role.
4. Interdependence directly correlates to the impact people can bring into your life and the impact you can create on other's lives.
5. Interdependence requires balance.
6. Invest in the right relations.[3]

The image depicts how the interdependent self is connected to all aspects of life. The business owner will carry issues from home into the business, causing risk. Conversely, the business owner will take problems from the company to the personal life. Each factor has a direct correlation to the many facets of life surrounding the business owner. Good decision

1.6 Socio-cognitive processes: Self-concept

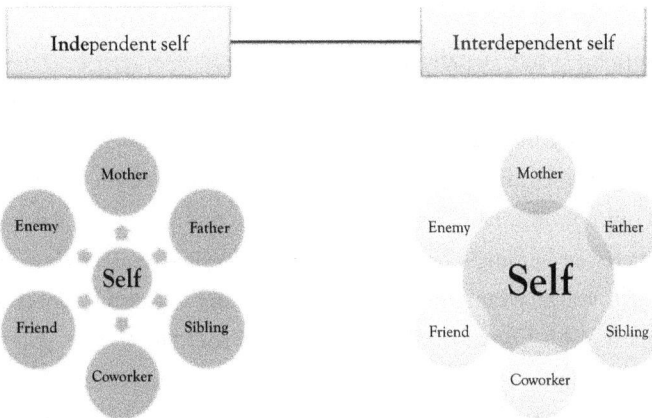

Source: Markus and Kitayama, Psychological Review, 1991

Prof. Dr. Holger Siemons

Figure 8.2 Socio cognitive processes: Self concept[4]

making includes the full sphere of influence with a deliberate focus on the ramifications for each element. This reality reinforces that decision making is a habitual practice led by meta-cognition.

In business, images of a supply chain make understanding interdependence very clear. Each portion in the supply chain serves as an essential link in the business flow. Issues with any one part of the supply chain create problems for the next division.

Business owners have a natural supply chain, as well. When a business owner operates as a sole proprietor, the business owner effectively is the supply chain. The business owner is responsible for daily business tasks, accounting, service offerings, business development, marketing, and governance. Decision making for each aspect of the business is at a premium for the solo entrepreneur. The business model, distribution channels, and operations hinge on the business owner's ability to execute. Interdependence can be ignored in this business setup. The action of establishing a board of advisers, a consultant, family members, strategic partners, and contracted workers is a solution to build an interdependent ecosystem leading to success. Interdependence, in this way, creates diversity and security.

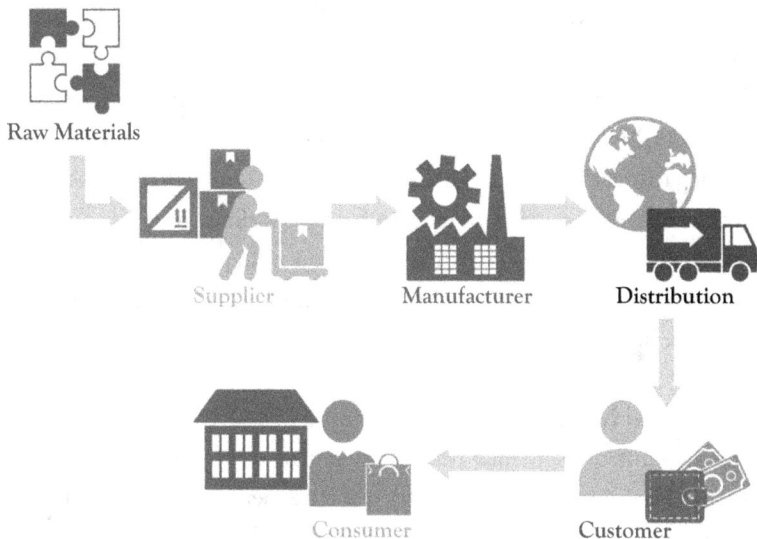

Figure 8.3 Business supply chain

There are three types of interdependence businesses can follow.

1. Pooled Interdependence

Pooled interdependence is perhaps the loosest form of the three. In this type of interdependence, each organizational department or business unit performs completely separate functions. While departments may not directly interact and do not directly depend on each other in the pooled interdependence model, each does contribute individual pieces to the same overall puzzle. This version creates an almost blind, indirect dependence on others' performance wherein one department's failures could lead to the overall process's failure.

This type of interdependence forces department heads, appointed leaders, and division supervisors to communicate consistently and intertwine the processes for efficiency. Manufacturing, e-commerce, and retail sales are a good example of pooled interdependence. The manufacturing company has to solidify the supply chain through international and domestic vendors. The business development department and sales team count on the efficiency of the supply chain to provide products for the customer base. The manufacturing sector depends on the business development department and sales team to generate sales for its revenue. The sales team depends on the marketing and commercialization department to create awareness about the company. All the departments lean on the administrative department for compliance, human resources, and payroll. If any of these functions break down, the company will suffer significantly. The decision making for the appointed leader has to include each department and the residual effect in the future. If the sales team promises quantities, price points, and delivery times to a customer to convert a deal, the supply chain has to produce them in a timely fashion with the appropriate margins. Errors on either side cause problems for the business.

2. Sequential Interdependence

Sequential interdependence occurs when one unit in the overall process produces an output necessary for the next unit's performance. Assembly lines are great examples of sequential interdependence. The demand for coordination to prevent continuous problems exist with the interdependence of tasks. Scheduling and planning your organization's resources in a sequential interdependence model is essential to efficient operations.

In the startup space, sequential interdependence is not only universal but the standard for scale. Tech founders embark on a journey to launch concepts at a significant scale. Frequently, tech founders need funding to accomplish their disruptive startup dreams. To obtain funding, founders must accomplish a series of interdependent tasks such as the appropriate formal structuring, proof of concept, beta testing, minimal viable product (MVP) buildout, consumer feedback, multilayered revenue channels, and a return schedule, to name a few. These steps are executed in a sequential pattern, typically based on need, access, and resources. Assuming the founder needs a substantial amount of capital to launch the MVP, angel investors or venture capitalists usually will not participate without the appropriate measures to demonstrate the business's health and strength. The business decision making for the startup founder stems from understanding all the tasks they are accountable for and how each aspect affects the next. Good decisions come by way of knowing how to position each task to connect sufficiently to the next task.

As an example of this sequential interdependence, one of my potential clients had a technology concept predicated on hypergrowth and the internet-of-things (IoT). The potential client solicited our business to assist with the concept development and the buildout of the platform. The business plan called for an application programming interface (API) with all major social media platforms. Sequentially, the startup founder would have needed a prototype to demonstrate the functionality of the technology. Legal and security measures would have to be ensured to protect the privacy of users. The API permissions would have to be granted and solidified. After conducting a thorough task analysis, the result was a mega-million dollar endeavor that the founder could not execute. Understanding all the steps in the sequential interdependence process made for good decision making.

3. Reciprocal Interdependence

Reciprocal interdependence is similar to sequential interdependence in that the output of one department becomes the input of another, with the addition of being cyclical. In this model, an organization's departments are at their highest intensity of interaction. Reciprocal models are the most complex and challenging to manage, one unit can change the rules and affect everyone else at any time.[5]

Graphic art, apparel companies, entertainers, and media are good examples of reciprocal interdependence. Small businesses such as graphic arts, videography, or photography depend on the consumer to create outputs allowing for sustainability. The consumer leans on the commercialization skill to attract awareness or connectivity with their target audience. Aspects such as logo design, color scheme, social media postings, and content creation are needed marketing tasks for businesses. The better the logo design and other specialization efforts, the potential for new business for the creator. The businesses that the graphic artist or photographer assists, serve as a model and testament of their work. Decision making is relevant in this space because the output of one business becomes the extension of the other business as the input. Supply chains, consulting, and project managers have this reality with the consumer as well. This level of interdependence forces decision making to encompass both entities.

Big Picture of Interdependence

As the collaboration between business units increases, resources and activities within business organizations become more interdependent over time.[2] How the business owner internalizes their interdependence and plans for it determines the success of the business. In my company, I am interdependent with my practitioners, strategic partners, wing directors, family members, chamber memberships, and company advocates. I have to provide value to each branch while growing the operation for the stakeholders. The best decisions come when considering each branch represented, coupled with its mission and value proposition.

To thrive in any market or industry, the shift from an independent mindset to interdependent thinking has to occur. The train of thought leads to considering each person's strengths, division, or sector and using those strengths to catapult the business. Individual business owners need their respective markets to experience good health to leverage universal growth. If the industry is performing poorly, the residual can affect the business owner. A significant business contributor in the space can be responsible for an industry shift benefiting all businesses in the sector.

Vision mapping is a technique used by my company to analyze the industry trends formally, substitutes, complements, threats, and emerging entrants in a space. We go through this exercise to assist business owners with their current decisions and future decisions and see how the other entities affect their business. For instance, the number of SUVs purchased in the automotive industry is connected to the price of gas. Electric cars are connected to conventional charging stations. Both of these aspects demonstrate the interdependent nature of business. A hamburger restaurant is directly affected by the sale of tomatoes and potatoes.

A prudent business owner pays careful attention to the ancillary aspects that revolve around the business and makes declarations. The hamburger restaurant's decision maker has to include the supply chain for condiments and side dishes before taking a hard stance on the position of his burgers. If the vegan population is slated to grow becoming a substitute for an all-beef patty, then an account of the new behaviors has to take place. The vegan populations' rise in consumerism cannot be ignored if the number of people is growing significantly. Good decision making derives from acknowledging all the interconnected and interdependent parts of the business and making provision. Current decision making governs the future actions for a company, and therefore having a conscious perspective of interdependent factors bodes well for the entrepreneur.

A decision to implement management control for interdependence helps the business owner to remain in order and supervise all aspects. Intensive interdependence exists when units combine resources and activities and engage in direct collaboration creating complementary aspects to achieve overarching goals.[2] Intensive interdependence can be transactional or cooperative. The association between new entities, existing business relationships, or potential industry partners profoundly influences all business dealings of the entrepreneur and small business owner. A mentality of interdependence recognition promises advantages for the small business owner through sharing resources and leveraging others' skills. The intentional recognition of the interdependent nature of business allows for identifying strengths, avenues, and opportunities from within and externally. Healthy management control of interdependence increases a company's bandwidth for execution, consumer reach, and conversion ratios. Whether transactional or cooperatively, each member has a vested interest in the company's survival and growth.

This chapter's meta-cognitive portion is to consider all the interdependent relationships, associations, connections, and divisions surrounding business. Taking the time to program individually for each one can be challenging but yields a dividend of enhanced scale and scope. Decisions within our company encompass the practitioners, the future practitioners, clients, and the overall market. As we work to improve our business model, we cannot be successful with our alterations or revisions without analyzing the ramifications of the members connected to the company. Good decision making always includes the impact on stakeholders and this process should be embedded into the train of thought.

CHAPTER 9

Why

The "why" of anything governs our position, perceptions, and perspectives. Asking this question surrounding all things increases understanding and wisdom, leading toward a more healthy and inclusive life. The "why" of anything is not a random occurrence, but a meta-cognitive activity exercising the action is faster than reaction train of thought. Business owners increase their operational efficiency and overall effectiveness when they quickly identify the "why" of any decision. Implementing the "why" question in the daily process increases the recognition of essential variables directly correlated to decision making.

Algebra is a mathematical branch involving letters, numbers, systems, operations, and processes to solve problems. Solving the problem is typically a measurement of a good math student; however, mastering the process of the equations is the primary focus. Perfecting the process will eventually lead to the correct answer. Conversely, if you do not understand the process, you may have the right answer, but you may not know how you achieved it. This reason is the purpose of the teacher's emphasis on displaying the work and awarding partial credit for a good process and the incorrect answer. Breaking down each aspect of the equation into multiple parts leads to the "why" situation. Once you understand the order of operations in the equation, the numbers are negotiable and interchangeable. You can apply the knowledge and rationale to solve any equation with varying digits.

Issues in life are looked at very similarly as a child poses the questions "why" to every response an adult gives. The child will ask "why" to the level of irritation and uncertainty by the adult. The aggravation occurs through fatigue or a lack of knowledge. Business owners experience the same fatigue and demonstrate the lack of expertise when posed with the question of "why" regarding decisions in their company. The intentional effort, interdependence, teamwork, and patience allow the business owner to expand the "why" concept in their operations. The "why" changes the focus of any issue and places the attention toward solutions. Solution-based thinking creates a broader picture of perspective, providing better decision-making opportunities.

The question "why" is not a question that is readily embraced. I have witnessed people grow in frustration because of the question based on the timing or who posed the question. Appointed leaders particularly can feel threatened or exposed to by the question of "why." Asking "why" carries the connotation of distrust and challenge. The question is a mechanism for learning and meta-cognition. Understanding the "why" is an empowering tool for more significant accomplishments through recognizing the interdependent ramification of decisions. The answers to "why" are accompanied by the aspects of confirmation, validation, and information. All three of these aspects are vital to the success of a business.

As a consultant, the first statement I make to a potential client is to walk me through their business journey to paint a picture of their current perspective. The first question I ask after the statement is "why" to whatever explanation they provide. I combine the comment and the question to illustrate a holistic approach to understanding their logic and ailments. I use what they articulate and their unstated position to lead the rest of the assessment. Without fail, the first statement forces the business owner to tell the story of their life or operation. The question of "why" forces them to think and re-evaluate their business offering with uncertainty and hesitation. This reaction speaks volumes about their train of thought along with their practice of meta-cognition. I have experienced this phenomenon with startup founders through Fortune 500 CEOs. The explorative nature of the question "why" sets the foundation for all beliefs, decision making, and actions. The lack of a legitimate answer to the question "why" a business owner's decisions and actions becomes sporadic and random increases the company's risk.

Parable of the Ham

A little girl was watching her mother prepare a ham for dinner one night. The little girl noticed that her mom cut each ham's end before placing it in the pan. When the girl asked her mother about why she cut off the ends, the mother replied, "I never really thought about it, that is how my mother used to make it." The mom called her mother and asked her why did she cut off the ends of the ham. Her mother stated that she never thought about it either, but she watched her mother do so. The mom called her grandmother and asked her why did she cut off the ends of the ham. The grandmother stated, "It was the only way I could make it fit into the pan."

This parable is an important reminder to learn the "why" of any process deemed necessary for your navigation through life. Spiritual beliefs, financial strategies, relationship behaviors, educational considerations, business philosophies, and health matters all stem from the train of thought employed by a person. If a person has no idea "why" they make certain decisions, they passively control their lives with unpredictable outcomes. The crux of good decision making is understanding the dependent variables of the decisions compared to all available choices. Merely repeating the behavior of others or mimicking actions does not constitute good decision making in isolation. Conscious awareness of the behavior and the action allows for the meta-cognitive process to lead the decision making.

The parable also spotlights the inefficiencies in the preceding generations as they prepared the holiday ham. The originating mother who needed the ham to fit into the pan found a solution for her problem. The next mother simply watched her mother's actions, followed her example, and the third mother. The issue exists in the value of time, unused product, and potentially mismanaged money. It is reasonable to think each of the mothers could have saved time, energy, and money by keeping the ham's ends. There was no indication or belief that the ham would not fit into pans that they owned or that the preparation time called for the removal of the ends. The reality is that cutting the ends off of ham may not be a major financial or time obligation. However, in business, making casual and poorly thought-out decisions can cost millions along with financial ruin for many. Human capital issues, organizational problems, and industry opportunities are predicated on the owner's ability to make good decisions, act quickly, and execute at a high level. Examining the "why" plays a significant role in enhancing the business owner's ability to make these decisions.

Practical Application of "Why"

The top two requests I receive from business owners is assistance with marketing and securing capital. With every request, I challenge their beliefs with the question of "why." Usually, I uncover other issues the company is experiencing, and the demand for marketing or money help serves as a quick fix option. As I assist companies with their fundraising strategy, I will test their understanding of the finances with the question of "why." One usual question I pose to new business owners or startup founders is, "Why would someone want to invest in your company?" The shocking factor is how many nonresponses or incomplete answers I receive. The business owner feels the need for an infusion of capital but did not employ a meta-cognitive process, including multiple layers of the question, "why." After completing an exercise of a series of "why" questions, we typically conclude that fundraising is not an adequate option, and more work is needed.

Knowing the concept of "why" is not reactionary; it is a proactive word. For example, when someone applies for a loan, some items are needed to complete an approval. All loans go through similar documentation scrutiny, whether it is an auto loan, home mortgage, or personal loan. The lender questions your work history, income, income frequency, credit score, credit grade, income ratio, and other financial obligations. The lender creates a picture to determine your creditworthiness according to their lending guidelines. This image helps the lender make decisions on your capacity to repay, therefore minimizing the risk. The person may "feel" they are going to repay the loan, but the lender is not operating off emotion, but the selected criteria. This criterion was created through a process by corporate governance through research, metrics, data, experience, and meta-cognition. Calculating the target audience's risk to generate revenue from one of the primary "why's" for lenders. The lender implements a system and a structure of interdependence to act as prudent stewards for the stakeholders. This behavior all stems from the original "why" of the lending institution. Small business owners must conduct their business in the same manner to increase their company's percentages of success.

Defining the Problem

The "why" is a motivational or macro perspective and the stimulus for the onset of decision making. There are many cases where a decision does not have to be made in the current time or ever. Defining the problem and analyzing if a decision needs to be made in a specific sense complement future decision making. The definition of the problem carries the thoughts of "why" is the problem, even decision worthy. People tend to make decisions based on risk–reward factors associated with their benefits. According to this approach, the decision maker is aware of the problem, develops the particular goals and criteria according to which alternative solutions to the problem will be evaluated, assigns the weights to these criteria, develops the alternatives, and chooses the other options that minimize the costs and maximize the outcomes for the decision maker.[1] The first aspect is the recognition and awareness of the problem. This statement is not to say that all decisions stem from issues, but they benefit from having alternatives in options, difficult choices, or dependent ramifications. The benefit or risk of a decision extends to the visible aspect of possibilities, while the value proposition determines the decision's difficulty.

Many of my clients face with what they deem are difficult decisions between protecting their assets through insurance or redirecting the money toward another aspect of their operation. The decision to forgo a legal assessment, buy insurance, or purchase a system is met with hesitation in the face of marketing, commercialization, or income. This decision always proves to be difficult owing to the value or lack of importance placed on asset protection combined with the premium of taking home more money or advertising. The decision does not happen in isolation but extends from the train of thought surrounding asset protection and management. Suppose professional insurance for business costs $1,500 a year. The extra layer of protection to operate appropriately can be challenged with thoughts of $1,500 in search engine optimization to drive more traffic to your website. The $1,500 could be earmarked for a new logo and website design. Owners may think to themselves, "I never had an insurance claim before, so why would I spend $1,500 on insurance to cover claims that I will never have? I would much rather spend my money on trying to make more money." The negative consequences of not having professional insurance may enter the decision-making process without solidifying the train of thought through meta-cognition.

Considering the decisions are not made in isolation, they are fragments of decisions made in incremental steps. The decision maker has a limited scope of each decision's entire ramifications, hence the decision has to connect to the train of thought and tightly held values. Using the same example, the business owner cannot determine if spending $1,500 on professional insurance will work out to be a better decision in the future than spending the same amount on advertising. However, if the value proposition is connected to the minimization of risk and asset protection, then spending the $1,500 on insurance is a simple decision. If the company is struggling financially and more customer conversions are needed, the owner may risk the protection of the company to reinvest in hopes of profits. In this instance, the need to grow the business is necessary and may not be a decision-making effort. Depending on the "why," the decision-making process may not actually be a process or undergo a formal procedure. The "why" could be a reactionary response based on social, economic, or situational pressures.

Recognizing the stimulus of an issue and the train of thought prepares the decision maker for the time of decision making. The incremental decisions connected to the values and the train of thought makes the "why" of a decision clear when a situational occurrence arises. This behavior creates an action that is faster than the reaction process for the decision maker. More innovative solutions, quicker decision making, and less experimentation exist when the decision maker is proactive in their thoughts and prepared for decision making. The exercise of defining problems ahead of time is a meta-cognitive action removing hurdles and obstacles before they become relevant. This behavior lends to speed in decision making. Although speed is not the primary factor in decision making, the certainty that comes with a sound decision-making process produces speed. When people speak of the benefit of experience, the familiarity of an issue or a situation allows for quicker reactions and movement. The experience is viewed as an asset for decision navigation. Defining problems ahead of time and thinking of solutions in advance is a pre-experience exercise aiding good decision making.

The "Why" Process

Examining the role of "why" is more than a mere question but a process of thinking lodged into the decision maker's muscle memory. The habit of good decision making includes an overall process that uses a "why" process as well. The constant redefining of problems is an incremental decision-making feature leveraging the rational consideration of changing stimulus and variables. The method of scrutinizing the origin of thought or problem circumstances provides a more sober perspective laying the foundation for objectivity. The problem becomes more manageable with the analysis of the definition of the problem and incremental decisions.[1]

Many factors affect the decision maker, but there are some basic-level factors to consider in the process.

1. Readiness
2. Motivation
3. General decisiveness
4. Beliefs
5. Information origin
6. Internal conflicts
7. External conflicts[2]

When considering each factor carefully, a decision maker learns more about their process and increases their decision-making ability. The readiness aspect speaks to the preparedness of the person. Is the decision maker in the appropriate position with the correct mental fortitude to make a decision? Many times, difficult choices surprise the decision maker leaving them vulnerable and caught-off-guard. By defining problems formally ahead of time, the decision maker has some form of defense, plan, and options management. The COVID-19 pandemic was an unexpected and untimely disaster for many business owners. However, conventional wisdom indicates that a national catastrophe or occurrence happens regularly, so a disaster plan should be thought of, planned out, and re-adjusted periodically. This issue is no different from a family having a disaster plan for their home in case of a fire. Although the decision maker does not know the type or the extent of a disaster that may occur, their mental fortitude and emotional state can connect to their mental readiness, placing them in a better decision-making position. The "why" for preparation is that you never know what uncontrollable factors may appear, causing a direct effect on your business, family, or finances.

The motivation factor is essential to formally implement in the decision-making process because it is the driver for all choices. A person must know what motivates them to act or not act specifically. If the value proposition of a company is the human capital, then a decision will favor the workers' benefit. If the value proposition of a company is the financial bottom line, then money-saving strategies will take precedence. The decision making is driven by the incentives selected in correlation with the value proposition. Just as our previous example outlined, buying professional insurance is a protective measure of prudence and risk aversion. If minimizing risk is a value, then purchasing insurance is also the "why" behind choosing to protect the asset. Questioning the "why" of motivation leads to a clear understanding of what aspects of the decision are primary in the priority list.

General decisiveness speaks to the overall propensity for choice tolerance and action. Some people are more risk-averse than others due to their traits. Others are more cautious and slower to make selections based on personal characteristics. The inherent personality sets the occasion for the decision-making process, train of thought, meta-cognition, and the "why." Decision making revolves around comfort and the individual's ability to withstand negative outcomes. One person's decision may appear bad based on the data or available information, but the personal connectivity is not taken into account by the outside perspective. This reality is when people say, "I can't live with myself if I make that decision." The personal attachment, regret, remorse, and connectivity to the manifestation of a decision is a strong force for "why." The belief system of a person is a strong influential force behind the "why" of decision making. When choice selection comes to a crossroads between beliefs and an opposite position, the opportunity for conflict arises. In business, ethical decisions are a regular challenge for appointed leadership. When formally studying ethical leadership, case studies serve as a baseline for habitual decision making. One typical case study is killing one person lying on the train track to save hundreds. This exercise tests the decision- maker's position on human life, ideas of the "greater good," and personal connectivity. The activity will display an unknown person in the middle of the tracks and then substitute them for a family member or a child. The exercise pulls at the core of the psychological decision-making process and the fundamental beliefs of a person. Some people have a foundational belief that all life is precious, and no life should be sacrificed, while others believe that saving hundreds of lives is more responsible and prudent. The reality is the belief system employed by the person becomes the motivation for the decision making and generates the position of the "why." Information origin is vitally important for logical or progressional thinkers. The range, scope, reliability, and relevance of the information is the primary metric for decision making. Bad information frequently creates bad decisions. People need to check their information sources and compare them to other pertinent sources for confirmation. This reality is one reason that board governance and team building are vital for business owners. A single-member company may struggle with reliable information if they serve as the only input source for information. The position could be jaded or biased based on a litany of factors. The board of advisers or the team of executives will assist with corroborating the information to ensure good decision making.

Internal and external conflicts speak about the pressures of the outcome affecting either the in-house members or outside stakeholders. These conflicts force decision makers to alter their position or select based on reasons other than their beliefs, value propositions, or what is in their best interest. An example of this reality is political voting. A politician may get accused of "flip-flopping" when voting in a direction and then running a campaign that may not match the original vote. In some cases, politicians vote on party lines to move a broader agenda. Even if the politician does not believe in the merit of the vote, they may believe in other aspects of a bill or amendment. This position can force an internal conflict driving the decision-making process. External conflicts create burdens squeezing appointed leadership or governance to make tough decisions. Investors or public opinion are often external strains on decision makers with high power. The decision maker will succumb to this power in the event the ramifications and outcomes prove significant enough.

The various reasons for the "why" of a decision are not conducted individually but collectively in most cases. A decision maker will encounter two to three aspects of the "why" when faced with what they deem are difficult decisions. In general, decision making is "a process of choosing among alternative course of actions to attain a goal or goals." In the classical sense, decision making is viewed as a process that entails two distinct activities. The first one is to decide what state of affairs is desired, and the second one how this state will be achieved.[3] Seeking the most optimal or considered the best decision is not usually found because of the number of variables and the associated unknowns. For this reason, "good" decisions are sought to provide the satisfactory feelings of achievement or progress. Prior experiences serve as a measuring tool for the current choices, while the outcome serves as the pass/fail grade of good or bad.

Self-Awareness and Your "Why"

The selected decision-making process must fit the comfort and execution skills of the person. The tolerance, beliefs, motivation, and stakeholder connectivity must relate to the mentality and personality traits of the decision maker. The self-explanatory decision-making process is essential for understanding and influencing the behavior of free-thinking decision making.[3] Current and new decisions are connected not just to experience but prior decisions with lasting effects. This connectivity reduces the merit of the current or future decision because of antiquated or irrelevant aspects. For instance, a couple may choose to stay in a bad relationship and eventually marry because they have been in a relationship for plenty of years. The sunken cost of the years together influences the current or future decision. The self-awareness aspect is to understand the uniqueness of the present choice combined with how the decision maker can make a difference with the new decision.

Whether a person is deciding for themselves or the benefit of others, the critical thinking process, including the "why," determines the individual's preparation during intense or complex decision-making scenarios. Self-awareness allows for a reflective view of how a person defines and qualifies their ability to make decisions. Self-awareness reduces nonconscious decision-making factors, such as bias and tendency. Decision makers must protect against these biases.

1. Framing—Options are presented as positive or negative.
2. Anchoring—Focusing on the first piece of information.
3. Confirmation—Searching for information justifying prior beliefs and attitudes.
4. Self-serving—Tendency to preserve or distort information to benefit oneself.
5. Self-justification—External rationale to support one's position.

The self-awareness component forces intentional action away from these bias types. A simple method to remove general bias is to navigate through the elements of critical thinking formally. These elements are as follows:

1. Point of view—The vantage point of issue for the decision maker.
2. Purpose—Specified articulated version of "why."
3. Problem—Explanation of the issue.
4. Information—Data, intel, and metrics surrounding the issue.
5. Concepts—Variables and aspects of the issue.
6. Assumptions—Common knowledge and believed attributes of the problem.
7. Conclusions—The possible result or manifestation.
8. Consequences—Ramifications and impact of the decision.

The critical thinking process is a self-awareness tool leading toward consistent good decisions. The eight elements represent a careful examination of any issue. The more a person goes through these steps, the greater the muscle memory in the train of the thought. A decision maker benefits from knowing their inherent bias and combining the critical thinking elements for a more holistic approach to decision making. The outcomes will benefit more stakeholders or connect to the overarching "why" of the decision maker.

Overall, decision making is a formalized process strategy that people must practice to improve. Decision making is not an exact science with a measurable result but an action of optimization and expected theories. Developing evaluation metrics and execution techniques do not reside in standard practice for people. The formal method of decision making is not a classically trained skill set or practice. Generating the probability of outcomes and estimating the impact of decisions is made easier through proactive critical thinking. The course of action comes from the perspective and motivation of the decision maker, coupled with the choice selection issue. Avoiding bias sets the occasion for the ideal choice strategy connected with the elements of critical thinking. People's experiences become the reference point of the "why," creating misleading aspects of the current decision. For instance, I have clients who decide against a sales strategy or a commercialized campaign because they previously tried it. If the result did not work out favorably, then avoidance or rejection becomes the new decision. This behavior is dangerous because it rules out the possibility of variables responsible for the failure or the introduction of new phenomenon changing the outcome. The simple question of "why" won't you try the sales campaign leads to the conversation of the previous efforts to learn about the errors during the last execution. The experience serves as a form of bias or misrepresentation of the current circumstance preventing good decision making. People must be self-aware of how their experiences shape their train of thought and integrate new modes of thinking in their meta-cognition.

The notion that decision making is similar to gambling or chance is also a misnomer held by many. Decision making follows a pattern more than random chance or circumstance. The patterns derive from causal factors associated with the issues or problems and connected to the habitual behaviors of the decision maker. The process of elimination is a pattern recognizing skill. In school, students take multiple-choice tests to demonstrate knowledge on a particular subject or aspect. The multiple-choice test does not determine the intellect or command of the topic but the immediate recognition of incorrect responses and probability. If the test has four answers and the student can eliminate two answers based on clues in the question or how the answer is worded, the student has a 50 percent chance of successfully answering instead of a 25 percent chance from the onset. The last two questions are broken down by the structure of the question and the material's knowledge. Now the student is no longer guessing but drawing on logical associations for decision making. This process stems from the question of "why" because the multiple-choice format immediately exposes a person who did not read or study owing to the questions set up. For instance, one of the selections is not within the spectrum of correctness and takes only a moment to detect if any participation of the material exists. This reality highlights the strategic nature of decision making and purpose.

Additional patterns in decision making is apparent in gaming, coaching, financial matters, and business strategy. Learning these patterns assists with the systematic process of decision making, leading toward a history of good decision making. The reciprocal of not learning these patters leads to consistent bad decision making. Comparing your goals, abilities, ramifications, impact, and the "why," decision makers can consciously and deliberately maximize their decision-making opportunities. The intentional nature produces clues about patterns in like situations and probabilities of outcomes based on consistent inputs.

In a football game, assistant coaches chart the progress and success of plays as they performed in a game. They are analyzing the success rate of a play call against the opposition's behavior, whether it is offense or defense. The coach considers how his team has responded to pressure, the execution of a particular block of plays, the time management, the impact of the game, and his players' emotional state. These aspects combine to form an informed decision on what play to call to win the game. Most people will say the coach made a good decision or a bad decision based on the outcome. The outcome does not determine if the decision was good or bad. The result is the manifestation of every possible variable. The determination of a good or bad decision is based on "why" the play call was selected. Some play calls are made without any numbers or metrics but strictly on the anchoring bias that they should give the ball to their best player, no matter the circumstance. Other play calls are made with external conflicts based on what ownership or a fan-base may want. Some decisions are made through a critical thinking process, analyzing every aspect of available data and playing the percentages. Once again, the "why" becomes the determining factor of the decision making. A single football play could cost an organization millions of dollars, a city could lose hundreds of millions, and an entire staff can be terminated. How these decisions are made carry substantial ramifications.

The question of "why" gives a broader view of how to adjust our realities through opportunity shifting, proper planning, and goal attainment. Regarding common sense, asking the question "why" provides more insight into what is considered common for a person. The more information a person is exposed to, the higher the opportunity for success. Good decision making is directly connected to the quality of the information and data obtained. What is considered common sense to a personal banker may not manifest as common sense to a first-time homebuyer. Having an open mind and utilizing your imagination increases the potential of learning new concepts to assist in the business. Making good business decisions begins with the train of thought and the metacognition employed by the deliberate practice of the decision-making skill set.

Notes

Chapter 2

1. (Greenwood, Lauren, and Knott 2019)
2. (Ma-Kellams 2020)
3. (Wai Li, et al. 2018)
4. (Thompson and Schonthal 2020)
5. (Da-ye 2013)
6. (Waglay, Becker, and du Plessis 2020)
7. Morning Consult (2019)
8. (Duffin 2020)
9. (Or 2016)
10. (EconMatters 2018)
11. (Merle 2020)
12. (Szmigiera 2019)
13. (Richards, Hamilton, and Yonezawa 2017)
14. (Kochelek 2019)

Chapter 3

1. (Keasling 2018)
2. (Zivdar, et al. 2017)
3. (Porumbescu and Grimmelikhuijsen 2017)
4. (Root 2020)
5. (White 2020)
6. (White 2019)
7. (Juneja 2020)
8. (Shmula 2016)
9. (Oláh and Popp 2016)
10. (Kothari, et al. 2019)
11. (VComply Technologies 2017)
12. (Orynycz, Tucki, and Prystasz 2020)
13. (SketchBubble 2020)
14. (Meszaros 2019)

Chapter 4

1. (Greenberg and Spiller 2016)
2. (Webster 2015)
3. (Weiss and Kivetz 2019)
4. (Mattingly and Kushev 2016)
5. (Issa 2019)
6. (U.S. Census Bureau 2018)
7. (Duffin 2019)
8. (McCarthy 2017)

Chapter 5

 1. (Lee 1971)
 2. (Schlitz 1980)
 3. (Bailetti and Tanev 2020)
 4. (Stroe 2017)
 5. (Schumpeter 2020)
 6. (Powell 2017)
 7. (Knight, Daymond, and Paroutis 2020)
 8. (Shu, et al. 2020)
 9. (Yan and Yan 2017)
10. (Van Ness, et al. 2020)

Chapter 6

 1. Holy Bible: New International Version: Retrieved from Bible.com
 2. Babylonian Talmud, Tractate Shabbat 3id
 3. Analects of Confucius
 4. Bukhari and Muslim, Sunnah.
 5. (Baker 2019)
 6. (Lauren, et al. 2018)
 7. (Belaya and Hanf 2016)
 8. Slideshare (2017)
 9. (Schmitz, et al. 2020)
10. (Bachmann and Kroeger 2017)
11. (Bai, Johanson, and Martín Martín 2019)
12. (Passera, Smedlund, and Liinasuo 2016)

Chapter 7

1. (Espino, Kozlowski, and Sánchez 2016)
2. (Al-Mataani, Wainwright, and Demirel 2017)
3. (Acedo-Ramírez, Ayala-Calvo, and Navarrete-Martínez 2017)
4. (Zhang, Liu, and Kokko 2019)
5. (Aickin and PKF 2016)
6. (Sandu 2019)
7. (Mankame and Bhoyar 2017)
8. (Hezun, Siri, and Timurs 2020)
9. (Corak 2016)
10. (Tinsley 2017)

Chapter 8

1. (Veerendra 2016)
2. (Frost, Vogel, and Bagban 2016)
3. (Bharatam 2016)
4. (Siemons 2013)
5. (Murray 2020)

Chapter 9

1. (Kolpakov and Anguelov 2020)
2. (Perez and Gati 2017)
3. (Topçu 2014)

References

Acedo-Ramírez, M.A., J. Ayala-Calvo, and E. Navarrete-Martínez. 2017. "Determinants of Capital Structure: Family Businesses Versus Non-Family Firms." *Finance a Uver* 67, no. 2, pp. 80–103.

Aickin, E., and F.A. PKF. 2016. "Business Many Challenges for Family-Owned Businesses." *The Northern Advocate.*

Al-Mataani, R., T. Wainwright, and P. Demirel. 2017. "Hidden Entrepreneurs: Informal Practices within the Formal Economy." *European Management Review* 14, no. 4, pp. 361–376.

Analects of Confucius.

Babylonian Talmud, Tractate Shabbat 3id.

Bachmann, R., and F. Kroeger. 2017. "Trust, Power or Money: What Governs Business Relationships?" *International Sociology* 32, no. 1, 3–20. https://doi.org/10.1177/0268580916673747

Bai, W., M. Johanson, and O. Martín Martín. 2019. "Dual Business Relationships, Opportunity Knowledge, and New Product Development: A Study on Returnee Young Ventures." *Journal of International Marketing* 27, no. 3, 26–42. https://doi.org/10.1177/1069031X19852961

Bailetti, T., and S. Tanev. 2020. "Examining the Relationship Between Value Propositions and Scaling Value for New Companies." *Technology Innovation Management Review* 10, no. 2, pp. 5–13.

Baker, J.C. 2019. "Transformational Leadership and Workplace Effectiveness (Order No. 13901861)." Available from ProQuest Dissertations & Theses Global.

Belaya, V., and J.H. Hanf. 2016. "The Dark and the Bright Side of Power: Implications for the Management of Business-to-Business Relationships." *Agricultural and Food Economics* 4, no. 1, pp. 1–17.

Bharatam, S. 2016. "How Interdependence Plays Key Role in Life and Business." *Business Daily.*

Corak, K. 2016. *Toward Better Corporate Governance in Small and Medium-Sized Enterprises.* Varazdin: Varazdin Development and Entrepreneurship Agency (VADEA).

Da-ye, K. 2013. "Six Rules of Persuasion." *The Korea Times.*

Duffin, E. 2019. "Median Household Income in the United States by Education of Householder 2018." *Statistica.*

Duffin, E. 2020. "Median Annual Earnings of U.S. College Graduates from 1990 to 2019." *New York Federation*. Retrieved from U.S. Census Bureau and U.S. Bureau of Labor Statistics, Current Population Survey, March Supplement (IPUMS); U.S. Bureau of Labor Statistics, Consumer Price.

EconMatters. 2018. "U.S. Consumer Credit Card Debt Soars to All Time High." *Chatham: Newstex*.

Espino, E., J. Kozlowski, and J.M. Sánchez. 2016. "Stylized Facts on the Organization of Small Business Partnerships." *Review - Federal Reserve Bank of St.Louis* 98, no. 4, pp. 297–310.

Frost, J., R. Vogel, and K. Bagban. 2016. "Managing Interdependence in Multi-Business Organizations: A Case Study of Management Control Systems." *Schmalenbach Business Review : ZFBF* 17, no. 2, pp. 225–260.

Greenberg, A.E., and S.A. Spiller. 2016. "Opportunity Cost Neglect Attenuates the Effect of Choices on Preferences." *Psychological Science* 27, no. 1, pp. 103–113.

Greenwood, A., B. Lauren, J. Knott, and D.N. DeVoss. 2019. "Dissenus, Resistance, and Ideology: Design Thinking as a Rhetorical Methodology." *Journal of Business and Technical Communication* 33, no. 4, pp. 400–424.

Hezun, L., T. Siri, and U. Timurs. 2020. "Corporate Governance in Entrepreneurial Firms: A Systematic Review and Research Agenda." *Small Business Economics* 54, no. 1, pp. 43–74.

Holy Bible: New International Version: Retrieved from Bible.com

Issa, N. 2019. "U.S. Average Student Loan Debt Statistics in 2019." *Credit.com*. Available at https://credit.com/personal-finance/average-student-loan-debt/

Juneja, P. 2020. "What is Kaizen? - Five S of Kaizen." *Management Study Guide*.

Keasling, T.W. 2018. "Improving the Military Decision-Making Process Through Critical Thinking." *Military Intelligence Professional Bulletin* 44, no. 2, pp. 12–17.

Knight, E., J. Daymond, and S. Paroutis. 2020. "Design-Led Strategy: How to Bring Design Thinking into the Art of Strategic Management." *California Management Review* 62, no. 2, pp. 30–52.

Kochelek, K. 2019. "The Psychology Behind Retail Marketing." *Retail Customer Experience*. News Features.

Kolpakov, A., and L.G. Anguelov. 2020. "Decision-Making Approaches to Contracting Out." *Journal of Strategic Contracting and Negotiation* 4, no. 3, 148–166. https://doi.org/10.1177/2055563620918811

Kothari, A., G. Kaple, S. Dash, and S. Phatak. 2019. "Implementation of Six Sigma Quality Tool to Generate Higher Revenue at Tele-Sales Department -A Case." *Supply Chain Pulse* 10, no. 2, pp. 10–25.

Lauren, S.B., T.L. Baker, A. Rapp, and D. Grewal. 2018. "Understanding the Long-Term Implications of Retailer Returns in Business-to-Business Relationships." *Journal of the Academy of Marketing Science* 46, no. 2, pp. 252–272.

Lee, B. 1971. "The Long Street." *Television Series.*

Lopes, S.C.P., H.E.G. Lopes, K.G. Coleta, and V.C. Rodrigues. 2019. "Business Models And Competitive Advantage: A Dynamic Approach." *Revista Ibero-Americana de Estratégia (RIAE)* 18, no. 1, pp. 90–105.

Ma-Kellams, C. 2020. "Cultural Variation and Similarities in Cognitive Thinking Styles Versus Judgment Biases: A Review of Environmental Factors and Evolutionary Forces." *Review of General Psychology* 24, no. 3, pp. 238–253.

Mankame, O.H., and P.K. Bhoyar. 2017. "Corporate Governance in Partnership Firms." *Journal of Applied Management - Jidnyasa* 9, no. 2, pp. 32–36.

Mattingly, E., and T. Kushev. 2016. "Most New Businesses Fail, But Mine Won't…Right?" *The Journal of Entrepreneurship* 25, no 1, pp. 70–88.

McCarthy, N. 2017. "The Top Reasons Startups Fail. Venture Capital in North America." *Statistica.*

McGee, A. 2020. "One of the Foundations of Marketing is Meeting your Customers Where They are, and in 2020, It Often Means on Social Media." *Shooting Industry* 65, no. 1, p. 46.

Merle, R. 2020. "Banks Reported Blockbuster 2019 Profit with the Help of Consumers' Credit Card Debt." *Washington Post.*

Meszaros, G. 2019. "What Percentage of Businesses Fail - The Real Number." *Success Harbor.* Availale at https://successharbor.com/percentage-businesses-fail-09092015/

Morning Consult. 2019. National tracking poll #190963.

Murray, L. 2020. "Three Types of Interdependence in an Organizational Structure." *Chron.* Available at https://smallbusiness.chron.com/three-types-interdependence-organizational-structure-1764.html

Oláh, J., and J. Popp. 2016. "Lean Management, Six Sigma and Lean Six Sigma: Possible Connections." *Obuda University e-Bulletin* 6, no. 2, pp. 25–31.

Or, A. 2016. "Consumer, Retail Sector Poses Challenge to Investors Amid Slow Retail Sales, Bankruptcies; Consumer and Retail Plays, A Staple in Many Private-Equity Firms' Portfolios, are Going through a Rough Patch, with a Handful of Companies Seeking Bankruptcy Protection in Recent Months." *Wall Street Journal (Online)*

Orynycz, O., K. Tucki, and M. Prystasz. 2020. "Implementation of Lean Management as a Tool for Decrease of Energy Consumption and CO0RW1S34RfeSDcfkexd09rT421RW1S34RfeSDcfkexd09rT4 emissions in the Fast Food Restaurant." *Energies* 13, no. 5, p. 1184.

Passera, S., A. Smedlund, and M. Liinasuo. 2016. "Exploring Contract Visualization: Clarification and Framing Strategies to Shape Collaborative Business Relationships." *Journal of Strategic Contracting and Negotiation* 2, nos. (1–2), 69–100. https://doi.org/10.1177/2055563616669739

Perez, M., and I. Gati. 2017. "Advancing in the Career Decision-Making Process: The Role of Coping Strategies and Career Decision-Making Profiles." *International Journal for Educational and Vocational Guidance* 17, no. 3, pp. 285–309.

Porumbescu, G.A., and S. Grimmelikhuijsen. 2017. "Linking Decision-Making Procedures to Decision Acceptance and Citizen Voice: Evidence from Two Studies." *The American Review of Public Administration* 48, no. 8, pp. 902–914.

Powell, T. 2017. "Strategy as Diligence: Putting Behavioral Strategy into Practice." *California Management Review* 59, no. 3, pp. 162–190.

Richards, T.J., S.F. Hamilton, and K. Yonezawa. 2017. "Variety and the Cost of Search in Supermarket Retailing." *Review of Industrial Organization* 50, no. 3, pp. 263–285.

Root, G. 2020. "What Drives People to Start a Business?" *Small Business Chronicles*. Retrieved from https://smallbusiness.chron.com/drives-people-start-business-20.html

Sandu, P. 2019. "A Framework of Family Business Professionalization." *International Journal of Entrepreneurship* 23, no. 1, pp. 1–8.

Schleckser, J. 2017. "The 6 Types of Power All Successful People Posses. Which One do You Have?" *Inc. 5000*. Available at https://inc.com/jim-schleckser/bthe-six-kinds-of-power-that-successful-people-u.html

Schlitz, D. 1980. "The Gambler." *Liberty/United Records, Inc.* Available from https://imdb.com/title/tt0080993/soundtrack?ref_=tt_trv_snd

Schmitz, C., M. Friess, S. Alavi, and J. Habel. 2020. "Understanding the Impact of Relationship Disruptions." *Journal of Marketing* 84, no. 1, 66–87. https://doi.org/10.1177/0022242919882630

Schumpeter. 2020. "The Gathering Swarm." *The Economist* 435, no. 9194, p. 56.

Shmula. 2016. "A Common Sense Approach with the 5s Tool." *Shmula.com*. Retrieved from https://shmula.com/a-common-sense-approach-with-the-5s-tool/18936/

Shu, C., J. Liu, M. Zhao, and P. Davidsson. 2020. "Proactive Environmental Strategy and Firm Performance: The Moderating Role of Corporate Venturing." *International Small Business Journal*. https://doi.org/10.1177/0266242620923897

Siemons, H. 2013. "Cross-Cultural Management." *Slideshare*. Available at https://slideshare.net/hsiemons/fh-aachenjune2013

SketchBubble. 2020. "Lean Management." Availale at https://sketchbubble.com/en/powerpoint-lean-management.html

Slideshare. 2017. "10 Leadership Tools." Available at https://slideshare.net/VALOZ/10-tools-help-hone-leadership-skills

Stroe, A. 2017. "The Importance of Performance Indicators in Analyzing Business Environment and Business Evolution." *Challenges of the Knowledge Society*, pp. 737–741.

Szmigiera, M. 2019. "U.S. Personal Debt - Statistics & Facts." *Dossier.* Personal debt in the United States.

Thompson, L., and D. Schonthal. 2020. The Social Psychology of Design Thinking. *California Management Review* 62, no. 2, pp. 84–99.

Tinsley, A. 2017. "Work and Organizational Commitment." *Confluence.* Available at https://wikispaces.psu.edu/display/484SU17001/12.+Work+and+Organizational+Commitment

Topçu, O. 2014. "Adaptive Decision Making in Agent-Based Simulation." *SIMULATION* 90, no. 7, 815–832. https://doi.org/10.1177/003754 9714536930

U.S. Census Bureau. 2018. "Median Household Income in the United States by Education of Householder 2018." *U.S. Census Bureau.*

Van Ness, R.K., C.F. Seifert, J.H. Marler, W.J. Wales, and M.E. Hughes. 2020. "Proactive Entrepreneurs: Who are they and How are They Different?" *The Journal of Entrepreneurship* 29, no. 1, 148–175. https://doi.org/10.1177/0971355719893504

VComply Technologies. 2017. "What is DMAIC Methodology in Six Sigma and its Uses?" *VComply Editorital.* Retrieved from https://blog.v-comply.com/dmaic-methodology-six-sigma-uses/

Veerendra. 2016. "Why Plants and Animals are Interdependent." *AplusTopper*, Available at https://aplustopper.com/interdependence-of-plants-and-animals/

Waglay, M., J.R. Becker, and M. du Plessis. 2020. "The Role of Emotional Intelligence and Autonomy in Transformational Leadership: A Leader Member Exchange Perspective." *SA Journal of Industrial Psychology* 46, no. 1, pp. 1–12.

Wai Li, L., Masuda, T., Hamamura, T. and K. Ishii. 2018. "Culture and Decision Making: Influence of Analytic Versus Holistic Thinking Style on Resource Allocation in a Fort Game." *Journal of Cross-Cultural Psychology* 24, no. 3, pp. 238–253.

Webster, S. 2015. "Accounting for Unmeasured Opportunity Costs." *Professional Pensions* 3.

Weiss, L., and R. Kivetz. 2019. "Opportunity Cost Overestimation." *Journal of Marketing Research* 56, no. 3, pp. 518–533.

White, S.K. 2019. "What is Kaizen? A Business Strategy Focused on Improvement." *Cio.*

White, S.K. 2020. "What is Value Stream Mapping? A Lean Technique for Improving Business Processes." *Cio.*

Yan, J., and L. Yan. 2017. "Collective Entrepreneurship, Environmental Uncertainty and Small Business Performance: A Contingent Examination." *The Journal of Entrepreneurship* 26, no. 1, 1–26. https://doi.org/10.1177/0971355716677385

Zhang, L., Y. Liu, and A. Kokko. 2019. "Does Ownership Determine Business Model?" *Sustainability* 11, no. 11. doi:http://dx.doi.org.proxy2.ncu.edu/10.3390/su11113136

Zivdar, M., N. Imanipour, K. Talebi, and S. Hosseini. 2017. "An Explorative Study of Inputs for Entrepreneurs' Decision-Making to Create New Venture in a High-Tech Context." *The International Journal of Entrepreneurship and Innovation* 18, no. 4, Sage Journals.

About the Author

Dr. J.C. Baker is the founder of J.C. Baker & Associates, "The Business Hospital". The Business Hospital is the only one of its kind globally providing Business Treatment to companies. As #1 Amazon Best Selling and Six-Time published author, Dr. J. C. Baker has written about logic, spiritual matters, and business leadership. With over 20 years of high-level sales, entrepreneurship, and consulting experience, Dr. Baker has been successful in industries such as pharmaceuticals, mortgages, automotive, education, faith-based, and professional sports. Dr. Baker is the creator of Transformational Leadership Exchange and specializes in organizational strategy along with process innovation. Dr. Baker received his B.A. in History from the University of Cincinnati, MBA, and DBA in Organizational Leadership from Northcentral University in Arizona.

Index

OTHER TITLES IN THE BUSINESS CAREER DEVELOPMENT COLLECTION

Vilma Barr, Consultant, Editor

- *The Champion Edge* by Alan R. Zimmerman
- *Finding Your Career Niche* by Anne S. Klein
- *Shaping Your Future* by Rita Rocker-Craft
- *The Trust Factor* by Russell von Frank
- *Financing New Ventures* by Geoffrey Gregson
- *Strategic Bootstrapping* by Matthew W. Rutherford
- *Creating A Business and Personal Legacy* by Mark J. Munoz
- *Innovative Selling* by Eden White
- *Present! Connect!* by Tom Guggino
- *Introduction to Business* by Patrice Flynn
- *Be Different!* by Stan Silverman

Announcing the Business Expert Press Digital Library

Concise e-books business students need for classroom and research

This book can also be purchased in an e-book collection by your library as

- a one-time purchase,
- that is owned forever,
- allows for simultaneous readers,
- has no restrictions on printing, and
- can be downloaded as PDFs from within the library community.

Our digital library collections are a great solution to beat the rising cost of textbooks. E-books can be loaded into their course management systems or onto students' e-book readers.
The **Business Expert Press** digital libraries are very affordable, with no obligation to buy in future years. For more information, please visit **www.businessexpertpress.com/librarians**. To set up a trial in the United States, please email **sales@businessexpertpress.com**.

www.ingramcontent.com/pod-product-compliance
Lightning Source LLC
Chambersburg PA
CBHW052109230326
41599CB00054B/5218